BORN INTO IT

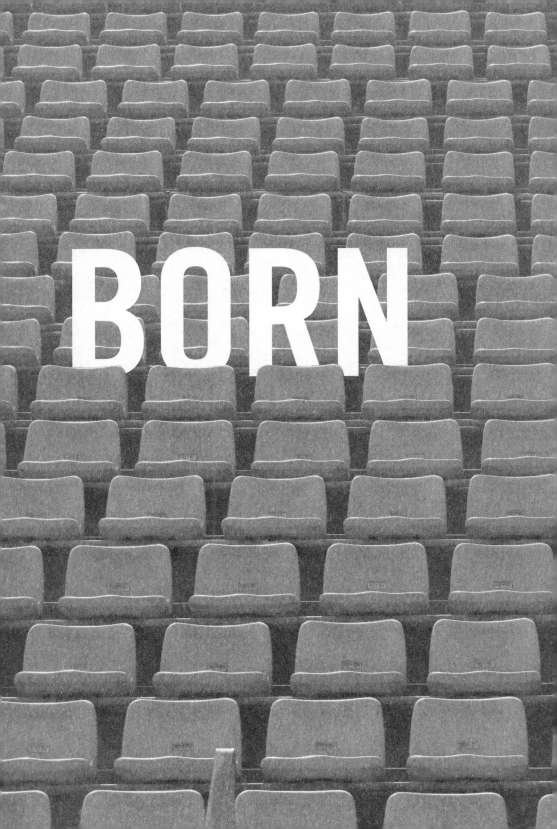

INTO IT

A FAN'S LIFE

JAY BARUCHEL

 HARPER AVENUE

Born into It
Copyright © 2018 by Jay Baruchel.
All rights reserved.

Published by Harper Avenue, an imprint of HarperCollins Publishers Ltd

First edition

HarperCollins books may be purchased for educational, business,
or sales promotional use through our Special Markets Department.

HarperCollins Publishers Ltd
Bay Adelaide Centre, East Tower
22 Adelaide Street West, 41st Floor
Toronto, Ontario, Canada
M5H 4E3

www.harpercollins.ca

Library and Archives Canada Cataloguing in Publication
information is available upon request.

ISBN 978-1-4434-5279-3

Printed and bound in the United States
LSC/C 9 8 7 6 5 4 3 2 1

For NDG and all the other less important boroughs of Montreal.

*In memory of my father, Serge, for teaching me to fight,
and dedicated to my mother, Robyne, for the same and
absolutely everything else.*

CONTENTS

BORN INTO IT

BECAUSE LIVING ROOMS

Because living rooms were our stage
And all our battles
Eternal warfare for subtle fighters
Stranger combat for tricolour soldiers

Because living rooms
Were our home
This time of ours
Is no time at all

This conversation is still
At the bar, and in the gutters
On the mouths of children and
Martyrs

We could go out
We could burn as high as the sun
And, still, I know you would say,
"As Winter. Be as Winter."

00:20:00

FIRST PERIOD

THIS IS HOW it starts. Equal parts anticipation and familiarity. We've been here before; we'll be here again. This is the start of a new season, and the continuation of a story we've been following all of our lives. It's October, and the Habs are back, and Canada can be itself again. Yes, summer is fun, and yes, we make the absolute most out of every second of that season, eating as many meals and doing as much of our socializing outdoors as possible. But this time of year, with its overcast horizons and cars idling to warm up, this is what we know. This is what we grew up in. This is what the world thinks of when it hears the word *Canada*. Soon it will be winter, eternal winter, and we'll all be able to see our breath, and there will be no end in sight, and our fortunes will be placed on the shoulders of men in sweaters iconic. This season is every season. This is how it starts.

We're at my house, or my parents' place, or a friend's; we are home. There is an understanding of loyalties; everyone is well aware which team we're meant to be rooting for. There might be a guest—somebody's friend or family member from out of town—a soul not of our tribe. There may even be a handful of them, but they are the minority, and any cheering or jeering from their side will be the exception. We are home, and our narrative is binary, and the good guys are our team. And our team is the Habs. This date has been on our calendar for some time. We all know that hockey dies every summer, only to be resurrected anew every autumn. As we get closer and closer to the season in question, the target becomes more specific and autumn becomes October becomes October 5, and soon we all feel—a little north or south of *knowing*—that there's a *very* good chance we will all be together, watching that game.

The day leading up to it is like any other, except it is informed by the expectation and obligation of something coming. What-ever work I'm doing, or non-work I'm distracting myself with, needs to be done by 7 p.m. Realistically, closer to 6:15. I'll prob-ably want to shower, or rather, I'll sort of think about show-ering and weigh the pros and cons against the pointlessness of smelling nice for men I've known since we were children. I'll definitely want to order chicken. A flurry of texts is sent out: "is there a hunger inside you?"; "did you eat?"; "pubes?" For whoever gives a shit, *pubes* is a sort of very stupid nickname my friends and I came up with for our favourite rotisserie chicken chain restaurant, St-Hubert. I'm not sure of the exact etymological evolution, but I know that we added an apostrophe *s* to make it possessive because we're Anglos, and somewhere along the way we dropped the "St-" and just started saying "Hubert's," which then became "Puberts" because we're stupid, and then it was a hop, skip, and a jump down to me literally just texting the word *pubes* to people. I'll get answers very quickly, as everybody I'm texting knows what night it is, and then it's time to attend to whatever other little preparatory tasks I might assign myself. Usually it's just down to rolling a joint or two and making sure the game is set to tape on my DVR, just in case. With chicken ordered and joints rolled, I crank up the volume on the TV and wait for the forty-five minutes of doorbells to come.

First through the door is Amir, who, though chronically late for pretty much anything else, is never late for these things. He says something about BIXI bikes, and then he and I launch into one of countless accents we've been doing together since high school. Tonight, we are cockneys and then, just as quickly, we are Greek immigrants. Twenty-plus years of friendship and we know of no other way to relate to each other. Really, it's either "Awright, guv?" "Yeah, fair play," "Yeah, get in there," or embarrassingly heated exchanges about the lamest possible subjects. Whether or not the UK can rightly call itself a superpower, for example. (Of course it cannot label itself such, regardless of its nuclear arsenal. This is what Amir and I screamed at each other about, one night in England when we were nineteen.) Anyway, he shows up and quickly takes his place on the couch. We're not assholes about that stuff, but still, it behooves one to get in early and make your ass grooves count.

The front door opens, followed by the muted sound of light footsteps, like a timid ghost reluctant to make its presence known. There's only one man I know on Earth who enters a house as spectrally as this, and a few seconds later, he appears on the threshold of the living room. It's Verdun's own Jesse, iconoclast, wallflower, and general inconvenient man. We performed sketches together at open-mike nights when we were seventeen, and for the past decade we've written together, professionally, as a team. Hands are shaken, greetings are exchanged. As he takes out his earbuds—each of us getting a tinny micro-dose of whatever film score he was listening to on his way over—and sits down, Jesse mentions something about somebody yelling in the depanneur parking lot.

On TV, the talking heads and highlights have been replaced by footage of the pregame ceremony. Players from each team take to the ice and do their laps. We all shut up for a second. It's not a profound hush so much as the first taste of focus to come. We haven't seen these players, in this context, since the beginning of the summer. And now, after the draft, free-agency frenzy, trade nonsense and gossip, training camp drama, and a typically underwhelming preseason, we're back and every game counts. Sort of. There will be stretches of apathy towards the end of the winter, but for now there's something of a connectivity, and we are all feeling it in one way or another. They cut to a close-up of one of our new guys. "Who is that?" Jesse asks. Amir fills us in, and from his description, we know not to be overly excited. Still, even if only by the slightest margin, we are all more excited than we were yesterday.

Finely tuned chicken instincts turn all our heads to the front window, and we are now all legitimately excited, because we are all legitimately hungry. A little bright-yellow hatchback has just pulled up in front of my house, and within it lies chicken that will soon be in our stomachs. I've been all over the world, and no one people seems to have as much of a profound appreciation for the combo of chicken, fries, and gravy as we do here in Canada. St-Hubert runs Quebec, while turf in the rest of Canada is almost exclusively controlled by Swiss Chalet. As of a few years ago, both bird outfits answer to the same corporate overlords of Cara Operations Limited, but their products could not be farther apart from each other, quality-wise. St-Hubert serves beautiful chicken, cooked to perfection and paired with fries and the single-best sauce the world has come up with. Les Québécois call it *sauce brune* or *sauce BBQ*; we Anglos call it gravy. The point is, it's brown and warm, and fries were made to be dunked in it. All of this deliciousness arrives at your door in an adorable yellow cardboard box, like some sort of old-timey chicken parcel, the French eye for presentation never far from anything in Quebec. Swiss Chalet, on the other hand, serves wet meat with pretty good fries and a sauce/gravy that tastes like soap and throw-up. Also, for some reason, it comes to your door in a weird, sweaty little biosphere plastic container. Anyway, we like chicken and are always psyched when it arrives.

My exchange with the delivery guy is brief, cordial, and familiar, as St-Hubert has been bringing chicken to members of my family since the O.J. trial. He can hear the TV, and our conversation quickly turns to the Habs, which is always welcome, especially during that horrid purgatory that is waiting for the little machine to process your credit card or bank card payment. Our little Habs talk, like many a Habs talk with strangers or acquaintances, reminds me that there will always be someone who knows more about this team than I do. There will always be someone who has committed that many more names of prospects to memory, someone with a more immediate understanding of players from an era that happened before I was born. This time, it's about something a retired Hab from the seventies said on a local French radio show, something about us being small down the middle and having no number one centre. We commiserate on this deficiency and lament the good old days. Neither of us is old enough to really remember the good old days, but that doesn't matter. We both know the interaction we're meant to have, and we play those roles. Like little one-acts, there are dozens of shared Habs-complaint routines strangers can go through when they want to relate to each other in a polite manner. The delivery guy mentions some prospect whose name I don't recognize, says he was very impressive in juniors. The path of least resistance dictates one of two responses on my part: "Never heard of him, but I'll keep an eye out for him" or "I agree and in doing so have become a liar." I opt for the former, which gets me a bunch of scoring stats that

I didn't ask for, and then my card is accepted and it's "Thank you," "*Merci*," "Go Habs Go."

Before I can close the door, my attention is drawn to a countenance both slight and familiar, his arrival marked by the subtle staccato of expensive bike spokes. This stylish little shit disturber is Evan, and he is every bit as smart as he is impatient as he is catty. He's wearing expensive dress shoes with no socks and carrying a bag of salad. He won't be eating chicken with us, nor will he really be watching the game. What he'll do is position himself next to the nearest electrical outlet so that he can plug in his phone, and then he'll just check it. Constantly. For hours. Every once in a while, he'll sneak away to eat something from a weird little snack station he has, for some reason, positioned away from the rest of us. It's weird and I don't get it, but we've all known each other since high school, and also, we're all fucked in our own ways, so no one really gives a shit.

Soon, the yellow boxes are open and we are all gorging ourselves on their contents. And for the first time since Amir's arrival, the living room is silent save for the sounds of us eating and a hockey game about to begin. There is an eagerness and an anticipation to all of it, even if we're only slightly more all those things than we were yesterday. We are psyched hockey is back, and psyched to be eating chicken. We are psyched, but we are also incredibly jaded because we are fans of this particular team. As much of a clean slate as the start of a season is for any team, it also just fucking isn't in a lot of ways. We can get excited that we are better in one

7

department than we were last year, but in the zero-sum era of the salary cap, every one of these improvements seems to be paid for by a step backwards in some other aspect of the team's DNA. Obviously, the cap is only partly responsible, as plenty of other teams have found ways to win a Stanley Cup in the new era. Our problems are beyond that. They are systemic, and systematic, and more often than not, they are the same problems over and over again. You could be dropped into the living room of a Habs fan on any opening day of the last twenty years, and I guarantee most of the fears and concerns and things to be excited about would be exactly the same as they are now. Our goaltending is good. Our defence is sloppy, and too offensive-minded. Our forwards are too small, and we have scoring only on the wings. We have some really talented skaters and some players with really soft hands. We have no first-line centre. Everyone can and will check the fuck out of us this year. This has been the state of affairs at the start of pretty much every Habs season of my adult life, and this is the emotional jumping-off point for all of us in the living room. We will cheer, because we can't help it, but nobody in the room actually thinks the Habs will get anywhere near the Stanley Cup this year.

As ever, we start slow. It feels like our boys were pulled out of training camp a week or two earlier than they had anticipated. The start of a season is funny that way: if the team comes out sluggish, it's a portent of failure to come, and yet, if they come out of the gate hot, the implication is that it's a fluke and the long endurance race that is the NHL regular season will surely take its toll, eventually separating the wheat from the chaff. It's hard not to be disappointed at the start of a Habs season. The off-season moves will never be as block-buster as those of other teams, and no matter what, we will always have our damnable history to remind us that our Habs aren't the Habs history will shine a favourable light on. We are children of the '93 Cup, close enough to the past to remember, but far enough away from it to understand what it is to be middling and underachieving as a rule.

We're being outshot, because of course we are.

The doorbell rings again, and I holler "Come on in!" to whomever is there. It could be a stranger here to murder me, but most likely it's one of the latecomers. In this case, it's my buddy Jacob. Jacob isn't a fixture at every game, not part of the canonical living room posse, but he's a dear friend and we all love him, and he really loves the Habs. He asks what the score is, apologizes for his tardiness, and mentions that my house smells nice (because it smells like weed and chicken). Jacob quickly finds his spot, and just like that, he's wallpaper like the rest of us, adopting the same slouched-back stoner couch posture, hunching forward only to eat chicken or when something interesting happens onscreen.

The other team has made themselves at home in our end, is passing the puck around our zone at even strength. We all shake our heads. Amir mutters, "Fucking hell." Jesse agrees that it looks like "they're on the power play." Jacob thanks the Habs for their efforts. It occurs to me that this is the default setting for all of us. Cynicism, ruefulness, disappointment.

We start every game from this place philosophically, every on-ice deed filtered through this prism. Maybe it's self-defence; maybe we've just been browbeaten by failure for twenty-plus years. I have a feeling it might have something to do with knowing how much better this team was when our dads were our age. We are all pre-emptively jaded and will roll our eyes, gasp, sigh, or swear in frustration at the slightest fuck-up.

We will also perk up at the slightest bit of effort or hint of inspiration, because as mediocre and 6/10 as the Habs might be institutionally, they are always one finesse move away from getting all of us up on our feet, and that's what happens on TV. Dump and chase in the neutral zone finally finds a friendly receiver, and just like that, the Habs have a two-on-one break-away that, for some reason, includes a spin at the end of it, which, of course, results not in a goal but a turnover, which in turn results in us getting scored on. Because the Habs are nothing if not made of infuriating brief flourishes of brilliance followed by inevitable defensive ineptitude. The Bell Centre is fickle, and there's a palpable shift in the energy of the crowd. That was a crappy giveaway, and we all know it.

The living room is all collective groans and angry gestures, each of us chiming in with "Fuck's sake," "Jesus Christ," or something to that effect. The anger quickly turns to analysis, and we all commiserate about just how avoidable this goal was before we all agree about who exactly was to blame. Our D was caught unawares and the bad guys went through them like they were water, but it was the attempt on goal that yielded the turnover. It was our forward. Our prototypically tiny, selfish forward, whose needless attempt at highlight-reel bullshit fucked us. The living room is quick to pile blame on this forward and dissect his underwhelming tenure as a Hab. He never seems to hit the back of the net, and he gets the fuck checked out of him every game because he's literally the smallest player in the entire league. Amir adds, "Also, aren't small guys supposed to be fast?"

The clock winds down and the Bell Centre siren sends us to intermission, down a goal.

We all get up at the same time to go smoke or piss, sighing and shaking our heads like old men judging teenagers. We're not even twenty minutes into the season, and we already know it's going to be a wash. But we are all romantics—we're Habs fans, after all—and our negativity quickly turns to an open discussion of what the Habs need if they want to make the playoffs. Rather optimistically, I contend that they're "only one or two big moves away," which is a dumb thing to say because that probably describes every team in every sport. It's also a fairly decent example of what it is to truly love a team, even if you know intellectually all the reasons not to. It's the romance that cuts the cynicism, the loyalty that tempers the disappointment.

And as we all pile out onto the balcony, darts already dangling from our lips, I am disappointed, and frustrated, but still somewhat hopeful—or, at the very least, up for whatever is to come. I am also with friends, at home, watching not just my team, but our team. There is a modicum of comfort in suffering this together, and in knowing that our icon, that of

Habs fans huddled together on a balcony commiserating, is one manifesting itself across the world at this very moment. We are, all of us the world over, suffering this together.

I feel comfortable, and this is all familiar. We, and countless other groups of friends like us, have lived these moments our whole lives, as our parents did before us. It's cold, and we ate food that was less than healthy, and we're smoking cigarettes, and we know some of us will be smoking weed, and try as we might to diminish or make fun of all the pageantry and patri-otism, it lands on each and every one of us in a very truthful way. We know the season has just begun, that there is a lot of hockey left to play. We know our chances aren't great.

We know we will still give a shit. We are hostages to our emotions, and holy fuck is this season going to be long as shit.

This season is every season.

This is how it starts.

BORN INTO IT

I REMEMBER THE red team. It's one of my earliest memories. I must have been three, or possibly four at the very oldest. I wander into my parents' bedroom. Dad's watching TV. He's happy to see me, and I him. My eyes immediately go to the TV. A dozen men are moving about on the screen, but they're not walking. It's far faster than that. They're not running, either; it's somehow even faster than that. And the way they move is fluid and unlike anything I've ever seen. They're all chasing something: a tiny black spot. Dad tells me he's watching hockey. And a light bulb turns on, my tiny brain expanding incrementally as I intuit that this is a thing.

When you're little, your parents constantly tell you what stuff is, and it either lands or it doesn't. This does.

"Which team do you like?" Dad asks me, and another light bulb switches on; my brain grows a bit more. I can now see that half of the men on TV are wearing matching uniforms of red and the rest are in blue. I then understand that there is a conflict at hand, that these men aren't all doing this together, nor is it every man for himself. These are two groups of men competing against each other, and I immediately say, "I like the red men." Dad beams and so do I, as I have apparently made the right choice.

I had just watched my first Habs game. Granted, I'd picked the Habs because red was, and still is, my favourite colour. But I also know that the reason I love the colour red is because my parents always painted my bedroom stuff red. Because they were Habs fans and I was always going to be a Habs fan. I never had a choice. I was born into it.

Whether we realize it or not, each of us is the hero in our own saga or drama. Each of us has a backstory: inciting incidents, plot points, and a theme. Much of this is up to us; some of it is beyond our control. My skin has an unpleasant pallor. I'm lanky and my voice is too nasal. I swear too much, and I'm usually too smug for my own good. I drink a lot of tea and my attention span is garbage. I like hamburgers. I like Joy Division. I like the smell of new shower curtains. I like Toronto's dedication to the day and Montreal's obsession with the night. I appreciate directness. I respect humility. I don't like birds very much. I'm a pothead. I read too many books at once. I fall asleep to historical documentaries on YouTube. I think I'm better than I am. I think I'm worse than I am. I'm proud, and hopeful, and angrier than I'd care to admit. I'm ambitious, and romantic, and usually feeling guilty about something. I've inherited depression, confidence, and a love for the Montreal Canadiens.

To say I'm a fan feels cheap, like it would be damning them with faint praise. It's more profound than that, more elemental. I love the Canadiens. I need them. I feel a part of them and feel they are a part of me. I can't remember a time in my life when I wasn't aware of their existence. Like my mother, and God, and my ability to breathe air, the Habs are eternal, and sacred. They have always just been there, and I never really had a choice. I was born into it.

Filtered through the mysticism of Catholic ritual, the Habs scratch many of the itches religion attends to. Emerging from a unique culture, steeped in history, filled with its own traditions, holidays, and rites, they are far older than me and will be here long after I'm gone. They are a means of dividing up my calendar. They are community, and escapism. They are my religion and, as for many a believer, born into a faith beyond my choosing, my connection to the Habs has been different at different times, tested and tested again. I have not been a mindless zealot, stagnating in my unwavering support and unconditional love. I have hated and raged and felt betrayed and renewed and fallen back in love with *les Canadiens*, time and time again. Just as many a Catholic, Muslim, or Jew has vacillated between devotion and nominalism depending on what's happening in their life, right in front of them. And like many a church, mosque, or temple, the Habs carry on and maintain, there if we need them.

My father was Jewish, my mother, Catholic, and I was

raised a Habs fan. Like them. For though they came from very different backgrounds and cultures, and though each of them came in with completely different sets of (sometimes incompatible) beliefs, my parents were both raised to love *les Canadiens de Montréal*. Ours was a house of two faiths, and my folks (really just Mum) made huge efforts to ensure that their children were exposed to each parent's religion equally. We celebrated Easter and Passover, Christmas and Chanukah. We honoured both sides of my family's respective traditions and everything that entails. And the Habs. Always the Habs.

It's not wanky hyperbole for me to say the CH is as important and familiar a symbol to me as the Cross or the Star of David. Because, though we honoured and celebrated our religions with the requisite amount of reverence and respect, there was always something transient or finite about it. Dad knew the prayers he needed to say on the High Holidays, knew them by heart, but that was more or less it for him. He wasn't anything close to observant. He didn't keep kosher, wouldn't be caught dead at temple outside of holidays or funerals. Mum was closer to being a practising Catholic than Dad was to being a practising Jew, but not by much. Dad inherited his quarterly interest in being religious from his parents, just as Mum inherited a driving sense of guilt and need for atonement from hers. Her parents were sincerely devout, and did attend church every Sunday, and Mum was educated by nuns for all of elementary school. This would leave a lasting impression on her that remains, in some form or other, to this day. My folks would split, and their respective faiths would be challenged in big ways. Mum would leave the Church and decide that organized religion of any type just wasn't her bag; Dad would practise even less than he used to. And with his exit from our home went the lion's share of my connection to Judaism. But the Habs? There was never any leaving the Habs. Never even a question. They were eternal.

Still, there were times when I wavered. There were times when I left the church, as it were. As a kid, I did what a lot of kids do and rebelled against aspects of my surroundings, and I'm sad to say the Habs were collateral damage in the war of independence I waged for the bulk of my childhood, most of which was in Montreal, with the exception of a fairly formative five-and-a-half-year period in Oshawa. Yes. Oshawa, Ontario. Somehow, almost half of Mum's family ended up moving to Oshawa over the course of the 1980s. And so, when the spring of 1988 rolled around and my father was offered the chance to move to the Markham, Ontario, office of Future Electronics, we packed up our Cutlass Cruiser station wagon and made the great Anglo pilgrimage down the 401. To Oshawa, where we would spend the next five and a half years, and where I was constantly aware of our otherness.

I was put in what was, in hindsight, a very liberal Catholic school. No uniforms or dress code, and Mum was usually annoyed at the apparent lack of institutional discipline: "Every time I go to your school," she said, "there's always a bunch of kids just running around the hallways, screaming." She wasn't advocating for corporal punishment; this just seemed like mayhem to her, especially having been educated by ruler-wielding nun-warlords. The point is, it was a pretty chill school that was, for all intents and purposes, a public school except for the fact that we said prayers every morning and attended Mass in the gymnasium every Friday. Which was also fairly chill. Our priest, Father Geniac, was old as shit, and seemed to fall asleep at every conceivable opportunity, and was always one line behind everyone else whenever he was leading us in prayer. Chill.

In addition to being very chill, Father Joseph Venini Catholic School was also very white. Basically everybody was Irish, Scottish, Italian, or Polish, and that was about it. Truly. I remember my first Halloween there, telling Mum about the different costumes the kids were wearing at school and that I didn't get some of them. In particular, I asked Mum why some of the older kids in grade six were just wearing normal clothes but their faces were painted black. That was the day Mum explained racism to me. She explained my father's experiences growing up where he did in the predominantly francophone suburb of Ville Saint-Laurent. She explained to me the awful, ugly, terrible things that happen when humanity lives like that. I could now put a name to the awful feeling I'd get when I was singled out due to kids finding out my dad was Jewish, or even because of my fucking complexion. This was early-nineties working-class Oshawa, and I remember getting chased home many lunch hours by this big-ass white-trash kid named Curtis, who was two or three grades ahead of me. "Fucking greasy Puerto Rican" is what he'd yell as he ran up on me, meaning to kick, or scare, the shit out of me. Mum explained to me how her parents raised her to abhor racism in any form, and that she was going to raise me the same way.

My dad's approach to racism was less about the principles of equality than it was his own reaction to having been fucked with his whole life. He was different; he wasn't of the majority, and the majority didn't want him. Same shit, different millennium. The difference with Dad and a lot of other Jews of his generation was that they stopped trying to get into the country clubs. The majority didn't have anything he needed, so they could fuck themselves. And, to echo a chilling refrain from when the unspeakable horrors of the Holocaust first came to light: "Never again." Never again will we sit idly by while you lock us in the margins. Never again will we anglicize our names and hope to be tolerated for fleeting moments of validity. Never again will we be afraid. Dad passed all of that onto me. He made me proud of my otherness.

Of course, it's easier to get to that point philosophically when, as different as you are, at the end of the day, you're still a white person. It was worse for other kids. I distinctly remember the day in grade five when Tristan, the first black student, came to our school. He may not have been the first black kid ever at Venini, but he was the first black kid I'd ever seen at Venini. His first recess, he was jumped by three grade sevens near the sandbox. I remember being horrified as they yelled "Black boy!" and tried to rain punches down on him. It's worth mentioning that Tristan fucking held his own. The three older kids couldn't get him on the ground, and he was returning fire right until the teachers came and broke it up.

As much as we like to condescend to our American neighbours and preach to them about the merits of tolerance and what we have convinced ourselves is a post-racial society, there are still sad, angry pockets of out-of-date Canada where being anything other than white makes you a target. I have no idea how diverse Oshawa is now, but spending my childhood there taught me a lot of vital lessons about privilege and entitlement. I wasn't marginalized every single day—far from it. A lot of my happiest memories are from Oshawa. Playing G.I. Joe in my friends' basements and at their cottages. Doing the thrice-daily Big Wheel commute back and forth between our house and the playground in Grandmother's complex. Losing hours in the rows of the video store or Gnu Books, our local second-hand bookshop. Fishing. Lots and lots of fishing. A lot of the best, most *Stand by Me* shit ever happened there. I was just always aware that we were different. Part of that was Dad's ethnicity. Part of it was because we were Habs fans.

It begs mentioning that the specific part of Oshawa I knew and grew up in was a very poor one. We lived across the street from government housing: white projects. It was the early nineties, and the country was in the throes of a recession, and we went bankrupt. We were poor. We ate meatloaf four times a week. All of our clothes were either from Zellers or hand-me-downs from wealthier families that my parents were friends with. We went to Arby's as a special treat. I never knew we were poor, never had a sense that we were worse off than anyone else. I think that's down to two factors: my environment and my mum.

There was no way of knowing how poor we were because literally everyone else we knew—relatives, neighbours, softball parents, my friends—were of the same class. If anything, living across the street from government housing, where I had a daily reminder that people were living off far fewer means than us, afforded me an appreciation of everything we had. But the other reason I had little to no sense of where we truly were in the economic food chain of Canada is Mum. My mother worked her ass off every day for over two decades straight, making sure that we had the best possible life we could and that we wanted for nothing. She made shit fun and alive. Even if we had to eat Kraft Dinner six days a week, she'd pour blue food colouring into the pot and call it "moon food." She always made sure we had something to read: "There's always money for books." She took full advantage of every event at the local library, and every day we'd do arts and crafts or meet a snake or learn about dinosaurs. What I'm saying is, she made metaphorical lemonade every single day. She did the best she could with what she had, and she hid the dire stuff from us.

It was only when we moved back to Montreal and I was put in elementary school in the cradle of Canadian old money, Westmount, that I even started to get a sense of our station in life. She also made sure that I never felt the world owed me anything, and that my fate was mine to plot, and that anything I wanted would come to me only if I worked for it. "There but for the grace of God go I" was something my mum always said to me, throughout my childhood. Especially if we encountered people worse off than us.

It was around grade four that I started to tune out from anything even kind of athletic-ish. The Habs, and pretty much all sports, were Dad's thing. Athleticism never came to me organically or intuitively. I lacked the specific kind of patience required to dig a sport enough that you practise it every day. I was always far more interested in watching movies and reading comics and coming up with fantastic worlds populated by crazy characters. After suffering through two years of softball—one under my father as head coach—I eventually screwed up enough courage to tell my folks that I hated playing sports. And as sad as it made Dad, he obviously couldn't dispute this fact. He knew full well what it was like to coach me for a season of softball, to have me start every single game with the same request: "Please, Dad. Bench me." Mind you, there was some stuff about softball that I dug. I liked hanging out with my friends. I liked the songs. For some reason, I liked all of our parents socializing. Also, I just so happened to be playing softball in the Greater Toronto Area during the Blue Jays' back-to-back World Series victories, and that kind of made everything feel special, like there was a movement to participate in. But I really didn't enjoy playing it. I would basically just live in the outfield, hopefully far enough from the action that no score would hinge on my decision-making.

So when I made my overture to my parents to stop putting me into organized sports, that was it. I was done. I had my out. I was not an alpha male, and I now embraced that and had licence to be me. In my mind, I'd gamed the system and life-hacked myself out of having to make any physical effort whatsoever. All I had really done was cloak my self-doubt and fear of inadequacy behind a veil of self-importance and artistic nerdiness. I sucked at throwing a ball, and sucked even worse at catching one, and I often got made fun of; having severed ties with the athletic world, I now had a means of avoiding being shitty and made fun of, all with the added benefit of "embracing myself."

The Habs became a victim of this self-imposed purge; I threw the fucking baby out with the bathwater. As a Habs fan, looking back, I couldn't have picked a worse time to bail. The Montreal Canadiens won their twenty-fourth—and, as of twenty-five-plus years later, their last—Stanley Cup in June of 1993, and it meant nothing to me. It should have. It could have. But it didn't. It sucks knowing I lived through our last two Stanley Cups but really have nothing to show for it, save for a few memories of my dad being drunk and sort of yell-singing, and kids at Venini one day, all of a sudden, turning into Habs fans. After years of being given shit for my CH-branded toques, mitts, scarves, and winter jackets—even if I didn't care about hockey, I was still a Habs fan "culturally"— I remember being in class one day and Marc Torcoletti coming up to show me some newspaper article. It featured a black-and-white photo of a bunch of Toronto Maple Leafs lying on the ice like a fucking crime scene. He said something about how shitty the Leafs were, not a good team "like the Canadiens." I agreed with him, even though I had no idea what he was talking about. But more, I was struck by this apparently random change of opinion. First in my classmates, like Marc

23

Torcoletti, and then in the rest of the kids in the schoolyard. Older kids, who had proven themselves to be bigots and despots more often than not, were now complimenting my Habs-themed Starter winter jacket for no reason. I remember being pleasantly surprised by all of this, but not enough to ask anybody why. Only much later, in my twenties, would I put two and two together and realize that it was all because I happened to be a Habs fan in elementary school during the year 1993.

It was also in my twenties that I fell back in love with the Habs. Head over heels. To the point where I became a season ticket holder at the Bell Centre for two seasons during a time that I call "the Jan Bulis era." During every one of those games, I would stare up in awe at the banners hanging from the ceiling. Retired sweaters from legends past. Conference championships, all Prince of Wales, from an age when there was no Eastern Conference. And, of course, the Stanley Cups. Like a living monument to all the greatest moments in Habs' history, the Bell Centre forces you to acknowledge just how magic this team used to be. As a twenty-something, I'd sit in there and get lost staring at the various iconic names and dates draped from the heavens. All of it seemed so far away, like victory and greatness were for Habs fans of a different generation.

All of it except the years 1992/93. Those years weren't far away at all. That championship happened during my generation.

I'd look out at the stands and see loads of boys and girls around the age I was the last time Montreal brought home the Cup, and I knew that none of it would be lost on them.

If, somehow, Mike Ribeiro and his immortals could lead this team to the promised land, these kids would live that with them. They'd love it with them, and remember it forever.

This was not the case for me; with every blown lead, ass-kicking, losing streak, or shitting of the bed, I, as a Habs fan, couldn't help but feel bitter and stung that I'd had the chance to know this team as it once was. I'd had the chance to know this team as it was supposed to be, and I missed it. I don't think I can ever forgive myself for that. (I can, however, forgive myself for missing out on the '86 Cup, due to my having been four years old at the time. I had a much different set of interests back then. Mostly Transformers, and apple juice, and remembering to wash my hands after I wiped my bum. Hockey, the Habs, a championship—all of these were vague concepts that I understood peripherally, if at all.)

We moved back to Montreal in December of 1993, on the heels of a Canadiens Stanley Cup win against the Los Angeles Kings. Yes, we moved to Montreal at the beginning of the fucking winter, and yes, we got there about a year before the 1995 referendum. As many of my folks' friends and acquaintances from Ontario liked to remind them, they were "going the wrong way down the 401!" That wasn't how my parents saw it. They made sure we understood that we were returning home from five years in exile, that other Anglos get chased out or leave in anger, but we left for different reasons and now it was time to go home to Montreal, as we were always meant to do.

I remember waking up in my new bedroom—which was, in fact, what would, once upon a time, have been the maid's quarters: a tiny-ass room located in between the kitchen sink and the pantry. My bedroom was in the kitchen, and the only reason I got that one and my sister got the normal-sized bedroom was because her room happened to be painted violet when we moved in, whereas mine was blue. Little did I know that my adherence to outdated gender aesthetics would lead to well over a decade of me living in a room that smelled like whatever anybody had cooked for many hours after they'd cooked it.

Everything was different. There was an edge, and a grime, and a maturity to the urban landscape I saw out my bedroom window. In Oshawa, though we didn't have much money, we'd lived in a brand-new house that we owned. In Montreal, we were now renting a nineteenth-century upper duplex in Notre-Dame-de-Grâce, complete with stand-up radiators, a fire escape, and a back alley that was an advent calendar of other people's apartments, like Jimmy Stewart's place in *Rear Window*. In Oshawa, everything kind of felt like the country. In Montreal, our duplex was five buildings up from the train tracks that separate NDG from Upper Lachine, and the whole place would shake every time a commuter train went by, which was about fifteen times a day. It was colder than I remembered it ever being in Oshawa, and I had no idea what a lot of people were saying, as years in the GTA had killed what little French I had.

It felt big, and foreign, and older than me. And yet, somehow, I still felt like I was supposed to be here. My parents had always made sure we were well aware of where we came from and that Montreal was our home. We always knew we'd return, and now here we were.

The city was still feeling the effects of the previous summer's Stanley Cup victory. There was a swagger and a drive to everything. People were cultured and confident, and shit felt big-time—at least, outside of NDG. Coming from Oshawa, anyway, which admittedly isn't saying a ton when it comes to culture, or shit feeling big-time. Confidence, however, was never an issue in Oshawa. The folks there may be many different things, but one thing they aren't is fucking afraid of anybody on earth. It's a super-easy place to get the shit kicked out of you.

I finished grade six at Roslyn Elementary. Every day I'd take the two city buses required to make the trip across Décarie and then north up the hill into upper Westmount, where, for the first time in my life, I had a sense of the class I'd been born into. Because, as a poor kid from Oshawa, now a poor kid from NDG—just barely, technically, still on the right side of the tracks—going to Westmount every day was a fucking exercise in what I can only describe as class warfare. Needless to say, the rich kids constantly reminded the rest of us how shitty our clothes were, and that bus ride was like a daily microcosm of how it felt to move from Oshawa to Montreal during that particular era.

The city was alive and so were my parents, in a way that I wasn't used to. The return home seemed to invigorate my folks, awakening them from what was an apparent five-year slumber. They were more energetic and sociable, and seemed to have an increased appetite for life. Mum and Dad each seemed to, all of a sudden, give that much more of a shit about their respective appearances. Somehow, the city, my parents, everything, felt like one big, angsty style festival—a party for heroes and rock stars, and it was already over; we just didn't realize it.

First came the referendum. If you have never lived through one of these things, count yourself lucky. In 1995, the entire province of Quebec was split in half, politically. These lines of separation are often geographic, but sometimes not. There are few sensations more unpleasant than having an entire way of life upended by neighbour being pitted against neighbour.

My family was firmly entrenched on the federalist/No side of the debate; Canadian patriotism was an elemental aspect of the way I had been raised since birth. The year before, my father had started a political party with some of his friends called the Canada! Party, and we had spent weeks following my dad on the local debate circuit. His party was not really a political party in the traditional sense: they didn't really have a platform and weren't really interested in winning any seats. Their sole mission was to remind potential voters that a Parti Québécois majority victory would lead to a referendum; that this was all the PQ had ever wanted, and that with the Bloc Québécois elected to the official opposition in Ottawa, a referendum would soon follow.

And he was, of course, right. The PQ won a majority in L'Assemblée nationale and shortly thereafter called for a province-wide referendum on Quebec's future within Canada.

The gauntlet had been thrown, and we were—all of us, on either side of the debate—made to believe that we were in for the fight of our lives. It was a scary year, and the closer it got to the actual referendum, the more divisive and less civil the discourse became. Montreal was littered with posters and pamphlets from both sides.

In NDG, there was a lot more *Non* shit than *Oui* shit. Every informal poll only served to cement the deepest fears expressed at federalist supper tables across the province: that the separatists might actually win this time. Nineteen eighty hadn't been just an anomaly; Quebec wasn't just a child that needed to tire itself out. We were scared, but we had just moved back, and so my mother was hell-bent on us staying, regardless of the outcome of the referendum. "This is our home," she said. "They can't make us leave. We will be Canadian citizens in Quebec." This was her refrain, but it was always cold comfort. I didn't have the same history with Quebec that she did. I hadn't lived there for thirty years before spending a half-decade in Oshawa. I didn't get to see Expo 67 or the Olympics. The Quebec that still felt quite new to me was grave, and binary, and the idea of living somewhere as something of a political protest was an idea that I was only beginning to understand.

On October 27, 1995, three days before all of Quebec would take to the polls, thousands of people from all over Canada took to Quebec. In what was dubbed the Unity Rally, whole convoys of buses from both coasts and everywhere in between made their way to Sainte-Catherine Street to let

Quebec know that it was wanted and needed. Canada came to say "We love you and let's sort this out." I remember being in the car with my folks when we saw the first school buses with Prairie plates, jam-packed with smiling faces waving maple leaves and fleurs-de-lys. We were overcome and touched, and for the first time all year, it felt like this whole thing might have a pleasant outcome. I begged Mum to take me downtown, and when we eventually got there and the giant fifteen-metre Unity Flag passed right over us, we stood side by side with Canadians from every corner of the nation, all of us there to prove that Quebec and Canada needn't be mutually exclusive. It is as darling and romantic a moment in hindsight as it was in the moment. I get shivers when I see footage of it. Tears begin to well up in my eyes. It is the kind of breathlessness and awe that can come only when you surrender to the majesty of patriotism.

This was not everyone's experience. For many a separatist, the Unity Rally was seen as saccharine and sophistic. It wasn't too little too late, as when the English finally started campaigning in Scotland in the lead-up to their referendum. This was foreign money that never gave a shit about Quebec coming to glad-hand *le peuple québécois* into submission. It was a velvet-glove counter-revolution. It was disingenuous, and it was also beside the point. Quebec's nationhood was never about how much people in BC smiled at them. It's a sincere and profound ideal, forged in the carnage of the Plains of Abraham, galvanized by over two centuries of perceived occupation. This rally was just one more tool in the colonial arsenal, like everything else the *Non* side had rolled out during the campaign. *Le peuple québécois* were fighting an uphill battle against foreign tyranny and capital, just as they had been since Montcalm lost Quebec in 1759.

I remember going to bed the night of the referendum, sincerely worried that I might wake up in a different country. My folks and their friends were all still huddled around the TV, drinking and smoking, consuming every bit of election data on every possible channel. It wasn't a fun night, like other times the grown-ups were all together in the living room. This wasn't New Year's, or Christmas, or the Oscars. This night had a weight to it, and as I said goodnight to the living room full of adults, I noticed that none of them were smiling and all of them were scared. Waking up the next morning to the "good" news that the *Non* side had won by a "majority" of 50 percent + 1 percentage point was like waking up the morning after your parents had a big row, the fallout of which lent a fragile air to whatever civility they might show each other. The issues were still the issues, and instinctively you knew they would manifest themselves in conflict at some point. That's what Montreal felt like. Half the fucking province was split into two sides of a debate that was always every bit as emotional as it was political, and the real result of this referendum was for both sides to feel hard done by and let down.

For federalists, it was a wake-up call, as if one was needed, a vivid example of what at least half of their province looked like. It was also a solemn reminder to all Canadian patriots that this country's heart was both its greatest strength and its weakest point. For separatists and Quebec patriots, the referendum was case in point of a status quo that had always fucked them over, proof that the vote was swayed by capital from outside Quebec and that the ancient weapon of the English races, legalism, would always loophole them into subservience.

A telling example of the divide that persists to this day, and will always exist in one form or another, is the difference in narratives vis-à-vis Jacques Parizeau's concession speech at the end of the night, during which he famously proclaimed that "we lost because of money and ethnic votes." These were words that rang out across federalist Quebec like a blitzkrieg, words that are still held up by Anglos and allophones alike as evidence of the exclusionary nature of the Quebec independence movement. It was seen as race-baiting and drunken xenophobia of the lowest order. A lot of separatists didn't see it as such. They saw their leader as having the courage to articulate, perhaps a bit bluntly, the centuries-old frustrations their people have felt: that it is their land and they are still second-class citizens; that only *le peuple québécois* should have the sacred right to determine their own future. Who exactly qualifies as *québécois* is just as hotly debated today as it was that night.

These issues have never gone away in Quebec, and even at twelve, the morning after the referendum, I knew they never would. Just as, even subconsciously, I knew that the issues dividing my folks would eventually tear a hole through our family. Which they did, around two years after the night of the referendum. It was, to say the least, a shitty year. One in which my faith in pretty much everything was tested. I understood the horror of watching my father break down crying drunkenly before me, begging me to love him and not believe the terrible things my mum was saying about him. I understood the equal horror of having my mum explain how long this split was in the making, and that she'd never actually loved my dad. Mercifully, they didn't do a lot of shit-talking or backbiting, but they fought and cried, and the whole thing just kept turning sadder and uglier, like a street fight that goes on about five minutes longer than it should. I was raised to believe in a lot of the old-fashioned shit, like loyalty and commitment and the strength of the clan. My parents' divorce savaged those beliefs and left me rudderless in that most transitional, self-consciousness-inducing era known as puberty.

When the worst of the fighting was over and the rubble settled, I landed on Mum's side. I wasn't forced to, I elected to. For many reasons, not the least of which being that she is my favourite person in the world and wasn't fucked up all the time. I had started working my father out of my life—or perhaps he drank and snorted himself out of it. Regardless, I was, all of a sudden, devoid of a male role model at the very time in my life when I was beginning to define myself. If there was ever a nadir in my life as a Habs fan, it would have to be when I was in high school. If the Habs are my religion, then this was my period of atheism.

I had stopped growing around the age of twelve and was still desperately waiting on puberty and a potential growth spurt. I was going to high school at a place called F.A.C.E., which was, as most words with dots after each letter are, an acronym. Fine Arts Core Education was the uniquely sincere, heartfelt, and very Montrealesque goal of this academic institution. This was after two years at the now-defunct Wagar High School, where I had a butterfly knife pulled on me during my first month of school. I then proceeded to carry a knife on me for the rest of my time there. And now, as Dad started to leave my life, I was plucked from the wannabe gang-bangers of Wagar and put in the libertine confines of F.A.C.E. I was small, and was now in a more artsy setting than I'd ever been before.

I was used to being the odd man out, and now I was at a school full of them. At first it was an emotional salve, a feeling that I had finally found a place full of people like me. I was, of course, a teenager, and my rebellion would eventually evolve from just hating my dad to pushing back against the art school equivalent of normality. Kids rebel—against their parents, against their school, against any authority. More often than not, these institutions of authority are intrinsically more conservative than the kid in question, and so it follows that when kids rebel, they usually run into the arms of leftism or punk rock or sexual libertinism. In my case, it was the opposite. I was at a school where progressivism and diversity were the norm, long before they became hot button issues for talking heads. I was in a class with three avowed communists and, at least for the first month of grade eleven, with four or five different kids who publicly declared their bisexuality. This was the norm, and looking back, I thank God, and Mum, for putting me in that school and allowing me to have that history in my blood. In my thirties, my beliefs have, for the most part, come around to what was effectively socio-political gospel at F.A.C.E. While I was actually in high school, though, it was a different story.

My rebellion turned me into a sort of Generation Y Alex P. Keaton. I made it my habit to argue on behalf of US foreign policy, capital punishment, and organized religion. I even started wearing little sweater vests. I became something of an asshole, ideologically. I was grappling for identity. It should follow that sports fandom and any sort of traditionally "male" culture roles would lend themselves to this period of conservative hawkishness, but they didn't. Because that was still "Dad's shit," and I was running as far from him as I could, identity-wise, anyway. Perhaps that's why at fifteen or sixteen I started attending Catholic church regularly. Every Sunday, usually alone, as Mum had completely removed Catholicism from her life. It's not lost on me how ironic it is that the apex of my Habs atheism was also the apex of my belief in Catholicism. They would almost shift places—I say "almost" because I can only describe myself as agnostic today—but I would need to leave home for that to happen.

When I was eighteen, I moved to Los Angeles. Kind of. I was cast in a Fox TV pilot called "The Untitled Judd Apatow Project" that would eventually be titled *Undeclared*, and my life was profoundly changed forever. I had been "acting" professionally since I was twelve. Those of you familiar with my "work" on Canadian children's shows like *My Hometown* or *Popular Mechanics for Kids* might be wondering why it's taken me this long to address the elephant in the room and talk about movies and famous stuff. It's mostly down to two things: 1) My time in show business would require a whole other book of its own; and, more importantly, 2) This is a book about the Habs. The only reason I'm mentioning it now is because my "career" moved me to the States, and that had a profound effect on my life as a Habs fan.

Like any teenager, I was eager to see the world beyond what I saw out my bedroom window. I was used to/bored with/sick of what I knew, and believed that adventure was intrinsically elsewhere. Montreal seemed out of step and silly; Canada seemed provincial and milquetoast. My first six months in the States cured me of all that.

My ambition had always been to become a director, even before I started acting. In fact, on my first day on-set when I was twelve, Mum said to me, "You want to go to film school; well, being on-set is the best film school in the world." And that was, in all sincerity, the approach I took. This is not to say I ever let my obligations as an actor slip in favour of furthering my raison d'être of becoming a filmmaker, I was just never a passenger on-set. I was a sponge, and quite proactive about picking the brains of whomever I could, learning as much about cinema as I could with the goal of quitting acting at eighteen and then applying to as many film schools as possible. I knew I'd stop being cute at some point, and that was fine with me because acting was always just gravy for me. I never needed it.

There was also a degree of fear to my thinking. I could chess-move what the next logical step would be, should I continue to be successful as an actor, and that would be to move. First, to Toronto, and then to Los Angeles. That was the path before me, and it scared the fuck out of me. Because I knew what LA did to people. I knew that every day there was another bus full of dreamers arriving in Hollywood like lambs to the slaughter, and I did not want to be one of them. I had always said I would go to LA only if a gig brought me there. It's easy to make that kind of random rule for yourself when you don't actually believe there's any chance of the "if" coming true.

Somehow, it did for me, and, before I knew it, I was the lead on an American network sitcom, represented by one of the biggest talent agencies in the world, and living on my own in LA. I was also a very young eighteen-year-old with no driver's licence and a crippling sugar addiction. My first six months down there were like the first night Tom Hanks spends in his new apartment in *Big*, or the second act of *Home Alone*. Eating candy for breakfast and being allowed to leave porno tapes lying around got very old, very fast, and then I was just sad. And lonely. Everything depressing was somehow exacerbated not just by being away from home, but by being away from home in Los Angeles, California, specifically. I remember flipping through the Yellow Pages, looking for the Domino's closest to my apartment, when I happened upon a listing for a local bail bondsman. In bold, above the man's name, was this sentence: "We specialize in spousal abuse!" Those words are seared into my memory. Something about them was just so crass, and base. In that very moment, I knew I wasn't home. Canada is many things, but what it isn't is tasteless. For the most part, we don't have cults of personality, or the culture of litigation that persists in the States. We aren't show-offs, and there's no place in the world with more show-offs than LA. It was like the Wild West, and my delicate Victorian sensibilities were constantly harried.

Luckily, I was surrounded by very good people, a lot of whom I am still very close with to this day. Such as my buddy Kris Brown, from Oconomowoc, Wisconsin, who, at thirty, had no reason to constantly bring me along for supper with him and his girlfriend—now wife—Aurora, or take me CD shopping, or listen to my insane ideas for movies on the phone for hours. Or my managers, Willie Mercer and Marc Hamou, both of whom are Montreal expats living in LA. They are family to me, and they looked after and protected me during that crucial time. It is because of them that I started to return to the Habs, because they're both big Habs fans. Willie, in particular. He literally watches eighty-two of eighty-two Montreal Canadiens regular season games. Every single year. And I was always welcome at his house for every single one of them.

There's something special that happens when you're far from home but surrounded by countrymen. I'm waxing patriotic about this because there are Canadians everywhere. We are well travelled and, for the most part, well liked. As such, there are little pockets of Canadian expat communities all over the place. We are Canadian, of course, so these communities are subtle; if you aren't looking for them, you'd never notice them. Because these communities aren't geographical so much as cultural, based around commonalities from home for which we can currently find no equivalent. And, arguably, the biggest one of these would be hockey.

I gravitated towards what I knew and understood, and started to get nostalgic about the old country, so whenever I'd meet a fellow Canadian down there, it was like getting to go home again. Sadly, I was also drinking back then, and I have sympathy for many a poor Canadian who had to suffer round after round of my homesickness-induced "stuff-from-back-home-that-we-can't-get-down-here" dialectics. It was all very pathetic, and painfully sincere. Eventually the conversation would shift to hockey, and I would inevitably be at a loss. I would run through whatever references I could, but would always end on "I'm not a big hockey fan" or "I'm not a big sports fan" or some other bit of nonsense. You see, I was eighteen, and stupid, and those were still "Dad's things." For some reason, it never occurred to me that I could watch and enjoy hockey even if I didn't enjoy playing it, so I had just tuned it out of my life. But now, being away from home, knowing the Habs in a different context, knowing that I was missing out on one more way to connect with my home, and thus myself, I was able to bury the hatchet. I could feel the swagger and pride that only a Montrealer can know start to well in me in a way it never had before.

LA never felt like home. I could never quite stomach being there for long stretches of time if I wasn't working. I couldn't really stomach short periods of time off there either, so I started flying home at every conceivable opportunity. Sometimes for months, sometimes for as little as forty-eight hours. And thank fuck that I did, because it afforded me a constant juxtaposition against my life in LA. It kept my ego in check, and it renewed my pride in myself and my family and all of our beautiful otherness. Things about Montreal and Canada that used to seem silly or quaint now seemed impressively genuine and real and deserving of my admiration. Maybe it was just a case of "You don't know what you've got till it's gone," but every trip home was like a fresh coat of patriotic paint, like falling back in love with everything I had always known, but in a new way. Like when you find an old box of books or tapes from high school, or a jacket you loved that you somehow forgot about and just recently found again: you love it for all the reasons you used to, and then some.

I remember the moment that happened for me and the Habs. I was home, high as shit, flipping channels on Mum's couch, sometime in the early part of 2001. I grew up watching a lot of TV, and my habits are reflexive: I have favourites I look out for, and I pretty much tune the rest out. I was most likely searching for either *Seinfeld* or *The Simpsons*, or else for music videos. Or potentially soccer. The point is, I was scrolling through the channels when I happened upon a Habs game. This wasn't a new phenomenon; I'd flipped past plenty of hockey games in my time and paid about as much attention to them as I did to whatever French-language round-table debates seemed to constantly be on. But this time, I saw the Habs and

I stayed put. It was a few things that got me, not the least of which was the novelty of happening upon something so specifically Montreal. I didn't get to do that in LA. I was home, and this was an authentically homegrown pastime. There was something sacred about doing what men on both sides of my family had done for generations: lying on the couch like a bum and watching the Habs with a buzz on. There was also nothing good on TV. I decided to watch that game, and I haven't looked back since.

In fairness, I remember very little of that game. I can't tell you what the score was; I can't even tell you whom the Habs were playing—like I said, I was high as shit—but I can tell you the exact moment I knew I was a hockey fan for life: it was when RDS cut to a close-up on the Habs bench after a goal. I don't even remember whose fucking goal it was. But as much as I was feeling the elation of the goal, it was the actual edit itself—the cutting from the wide shot of the ice to the scorer sitting back down and smiling—that did it for me. I remember thinking, *I remember this*. I remembered this sensation, this sequence of events: the Habs score, the crowd cheers, and so does our living room; then we watch the replay; then the scorer sits down; then they cut to a close-up of him. This was the stanza, repeated countless times, night after night, year after year, in living rooms across the country. This was Canada, in a math and music specific to herself, and I was a part of it.

It helps that hockey is the greatest sport the world has ever come up with. I say this with no authority other than the pride of the convert, or the gratitude of the prodigal son. It is faster, meaner, more brutal, and more elegant than any other game in existence. It is also a sport populated by far fewer assholes and high school bullies than any other. It is truly a team sport, and individuality is a necessary evil, not a model to be emulated. It is tough, and strong, and patient, and humble. It is a physical manifestation of all the best bits of being Canadian, if such a thing actually exists.

My connection to the game quickly blossomed from intellectual interest to emotional attachment, and it all became very intense, very quickly. I followed every Habs game I could, whenever and wherever I could. Often on a laptop in a trailer on-set in God-knows-where, New Mexico, either watching an illegal link or just listening to CJAD or TSN 690 radio online. My calendar quickly filled up with entertainment, and it was like my lifetime of knowing the Habs peripherally and academically—I always knew all the important names from Habs history and all the big stats—was in preparation for getting to enjoy them as a grown-up. I was returning to the religion of my youth. I was being born again. Like many a convert, my regained or new-found faith bled into all aspects of my life, to the point where I became a season ticket holder at the Bell Centre for two seasons and went to almost every Habs game at the Staples Center in LA over the next decade and a half.

The Habs would become as fundamental a part of my life as my family, along with all that entails, for better or worse. They would become everything from how I divvy up my week to a painful reminder of everything fucked in my life. I would learn what it is like to watch every game of a season, only to not make the playoffs, and what it is like to march down René-Lévesque, one of thousands upon thousands of fans, all of us clad in the same colours, celebrating the same victory. I would know what it is like to watch P.K. score against Boston in game 7, sending the game to OT, cheering silently with my then fiancée in a tiny Manhattan apartment, watching the game two hours after the fact because her play only ended at 10 p.m. I would know what it is like to have the sound of play-by-play announcers break my heart in two because it served as a reminder of a marriage that wasn't to be.

My love for the Habs ebbs and flows; some seasons I am more heavily invested than others, but the team will endure and so will my connection to them, as all roads will always lead me back to Montreal. The Montreal Canadiens are in me, as they've always been. It just took me a while to acknowledge it. I suppose that doesn't matter, because I was born into it.

It's not just that I was raised to love them, it's that I still love them. They mean more to me, in different ways, than they used to. The world is a kaleidoscope of transient personalities, and the Habs give me a means of expressing and identifying myself. Being a Habs fan affords me a language to tell the world: This is me. This is where I come from. This is what I find important, or at least worthy of my time. This is the history to which I connect and contribute. This is my tribe, and this is my clan. This is my context. That's all any of it really is: context. When you make an outward display of appreciation for anything—a team, heritage, nationality, faith, philosophy, band, family name, political party—you are choosing the context in which you would like to viewed. I want the world to know, and for history to reflect, that this is what I think is important.

Researching and embracing my ancestral histories through the family tree I've spent the bulk of the last decade building, I have been given the chance to understand who I am by understanding where I come from. I get dozens of piecemeal, fragmented glimpses into the triumphs, tragedies, and everyday concerns of my ancestors. In experiencing these portions of their narratives, preserved in census forms and other vessels of cold data, I get that much more perspective on my own. I understand the narrative I am inheriting, and that understanding informs how I present myself to the world. Their narratives give me a connection to something ancient in the young, postmodern country in which I was born. And it's the same with the Habs. I've always known that I was a Habs fan, just as I've always known what family I belonged to. But now I lean into it, I embrace it and let it inform my interests and tastes. Just as pride in my family was only compounded by research into our history, my love of the Habs has only ever been renewed by the time I've spent researching the heady past from whence the Habs sprang forth.

The Habs also give me a way to connect with people. For whatever reasons, I have always been wired differently, always felt like a bit of an outsider. Maybe it's my hodgepodge ethnic background, or maybe it's my anemia, but I have always been a homebody and I have always just liked what I liked and dis-liked or dismissed everything else. As such, I have spent my life constantly aware of cultural phenomena that mean little or nothing to me. I've watched from afar as the world seemed to be in on a joke that I just didn't get. Incidentally, it only seems to be getting worse with age. When I was younger, even if I didn't give a shit, at least I knew what everybody was talking about. Now, it seems like every day carries with it a whole new slew of references that seem increasingly like gibberish, and somehow I'm already crabbier than either of my grandads ever were. The point is, I'm used to missing out on stuff that loads of people enjoy, and the Habs give me a remedy to that. They give me a community. They give me belonging. They give me the joy of a shared experience. They give me a reason to have people over and, sometimes, a reason to leave the house. They give me something to talk about. They give me something normal. Like I was the kid my dad was supposed to have; like I was the kid that was in every other house on our block. Like I was never picked last, or chased home for being the darkest kid at school. It makes me feel a part of a world in which I have always felt like some-thing of a tourist.

But really, more than anything, the Habs are my team. They are my team, and try as I might, I will never quit them completely. As much as my faith is constantly tested by bad trades and boring coaching decisions, as much as my love for them is sometimes spoiled by someone or something else— like living with someone and having them fall in love with the Habs as they fall in love with you, and then it ends and what was once your thing is now "our thing," and there is no "our" and now you're fucked—I will always come back. The bad stuff will pass. The negative neuro-association will fade in time. The Habs will be the Habs no matter what, and for better or worse, I will always be a Habs fan.

Because I never had a choice.

I was born into it.

DAD

IT WAS CHRISTMAS Eve, 1995. It snowed that night. It usually does in Montreal. In general and on Christmas Eve specifically. Mum was nursing her one Baileys of the year as she read us "The Night Before Christmas." My sister, Taylor, was curled up next to her on the couch, while I was cozy in an armchair, each of us sipping hot chocolate as we listened intently. Cats purred as they circled our feet. The fire crackled and roared in its place. Basically, picture the coziest Norman Rockwell painting you can think of and then imagine admiring it while sitting in the Friendly Giant's little rocking chair as Donald Sutherland talks about blankets, and you might begin to understand how cozy we were in our living room that night. We, of course, being the aforementioned Mum, Taylor, and I. My father was in my parents' room, watching the Habs.

Mum took a sip and began, "'Twas the night before Christmas, and all through the house," but no sooner did those immortal words leave her mouth than my father chimed in from down the hall with: "Jesus fucking Christ!" My sister and I, obviously, burst into laughter. I seem to remember my mother also finding it funny, but as she would go on to divorce my father a year or so later, she may not have found it quite as hilarious as we did. Mum continued, or at least tried her best to: ". . . not a creature was stirring, not even a mouse." Through drywall and wood, and with noticeably comic timing, Dad bellowed, "Goddammit! You lazy fucks!" or something folksy like that. Unbeknownst to him, Dad was, literally, punctuating each stanza of North America's favourite holiday poem with the particular kind of vitriol and swearing that only the Habs can trigger.

This is not to say that my father wasn't normally filled with vitriol and swearing. He was! But there was a specific contempt he reserved for the Habs when he thought they weren't doing what they were meant to do or being as good as they could be.

Growing up a Jewish immigrant in a predominantly Québécois neighbourhood—Ville Saint-Laurent, for whoever cares—during the fifties and sixties, Dad seemed to have distilled everyday living down to two binary options: be hard or get taken advantage of. His family had come to Canada via Paris. His mother was from Normandy; his father, an Italian-speaking Jew from Egypt. Dad looked different, and he had a funny accent, and his family didn't go to church like the other families on his block. Inevitably, this would lead to conflict of some kind, and Dad decided, at a very early age, that he wasn't going to be anybody's victim. He fought. With an intensity born of both first-generation anxieties and a small-man complex, Dad took on all comers. Whether they be the gentile members of an opposing hockey team— some parents of whom would literally rain pennies down on my dad and the other members of the Beth-El Wings as they skated onto the ice—or bikers ogling his Magen David, which was, of course, big as shit and very visible through a shirt unbuttoned to his navel, he fought everybody. He got his ass kicked plenty of times too, but that was hardly the point. Just keep fighting. If for no other reason than "Fuck that guy." Dad had the fight in him. He just liked it. He never stopped, either. He fought right up until he died in 2004 at the age of forty-nine.

Like many a new Canadian, Dad found a connection to local culture through hockey: playing it, which he did his whole life, and just as, if not more, importantly, watching, listening to, and reading about *les Canadiens de Montréal*. As a child, he fell in love with the mythos of titans like the Rocket and Le Gros Bill, each of them every bit as colourful and superhuman as his favourite comic-book heroes Shazam and Superman. As a teenager and young man, he idolized long-haired poet-outlaws like Shutt, Robinson, Gainey, Savard. Ken Dryden, the boy-scribe and goaltending prodigy. Guy fucking Lafleur: the very apotheosis of flamboyant 1970s Montreal excess and charisma.

To come of age during that particular generation, in that particular city, as my dad did, was to come by Habs fandom about as honestly as one could. Baby-boomer optimism and the first sparks of Quiet Revolution sentiment imbued both the city and her one true team with an elemental energy that would carry on for the next quarter-century or so, manifested in flashpoints and movements like the Habs dynasty of the fifties, which gave us the Richard Riot; the Leafs rivalry of the sixties; Expo 67; John and Yoko recording "Give Peace a Chance" naked in their hotel room at the Queen Elizabeth; years of bombings escalating in severity and culminating with the October Crisis; *"Da, da, Canada! Nyet, nyet, Soviet!"* and the 1972 Summit Series; the Habs dynasty of the seventies, featuring the 1976/77 team, arguably the single best hockey team in history; the 1976 Summer Olympics; the dawn of the Super Series and the legend of the New Year's Eve game against the Red Army.

It was one brief era-electric when Montreal flirted with cosmopolitanism and marked the pages of history with her every move. And to be sure, there were moments, however fleeting they might have been, when Montreal actually achieved greatness only to then reveal herself as her own worst enemy, time and time again. Just like my father. And like his beloved Montreal, my father, Serge Baruchel, was very much of a time.

My father started doing drugs when he was fourteen. He started dealing them when he was around fifteen or sixteen. Weed at first, then cocaine; same order in both scenarios. I'd venture to say that, after or possibly even alongside the Habs, drug life was Dad's first true love, one he would never get over. He loved that shit. Doing coke. Selling it. All of it. He loved being a bad guy as much as he loved being fucked up. He raced the devil continuously from age fourteen on, always with the welcome weight of a monkey on his back. Everything and everyone else would take a back seat. Always. The Habs, Mum, Taylor, and me included.

He wouldn't have seen it that way, of course, because he was a drunk and a drug addict and believed he could pull it off. He believed he could function. He believed he was the one fucking guy who didn't have to make the unpleasant choice between being a drug addict and having a family. Obviously, he was wrong. He would go on to know this and know it hard, but like many a drunk and drug addict, it would be far too late and the end would come before he was ready. Back at the beginning, however, when he first met "Mary Jane" and "Charlie," everything was rock and roll and the invincibility of youth.

At the beginning, everything was the 1970s. Dad would never be more current than he was then. He was slick and tough and had the gift of the gab; he was one of those dialectal chameleons who can, will, and even must adopt the accent of whomever they're speaking to. He was playing hockey and studying kung fu and getting fucked up and running with gangsters. He was picking fights and playing with guns, and he thought everybody was a sucker. He loved Bruce Lee and dressed like Eric Clapton, and he never gave a sucker an even break. He smuggled yayo out of Colombia and always fasted on Yom Kippur. He never waited in line. He knew good music, and what was funny, and was always up to date on what the trendsetters were doing down in the States. As I say, he was racing the devil, and hating his father, and burning like napalm, and he watched the Habs win five Stanley Cups.

Under the guidance of the single greatest coach in the history of hockey, Verdun's own Scotty Bowman, those players were living history through every shift of every period. Young and electric, and every bit as idiosyncratically confident as Montreal herself, the seventies Habs seemed to embody the spirit and character of this transitional era. Or, at the very least, they embodied the spirit and character that my dad believed was in him. They were young and ambitious and proud. They were a distillation of the most aspirational masculine attributes of both counterculture and traditionalism. They would play as hard as they partied. They were motivated by glory and guilty consciences. They were distinct and high on themselves, and they won sixty games in an eighty-game season in which they suffered only one defeat! They were alive and they wanted the world. Just like my father. And just like my father, the next quarter-decade would hold a slow-dripping disappointment, a downward spiral, interrupted by two great victories. For the next quarter-decade, the Habs, and my father, would be chasing their own ghosts, doing everything they could to find a way back to, or to recreate, that halcyon era when everything was the way it was supposed to be.

My mother, Robyne, met my father, Serge, at a nightclub in the autumn of 1979. Club 1234 on Rue de la Montagne, to be specific. She was twenty-five, and beautiful. Having been on her own in the big city since she was seventeen, Mum was dividing her time fairly equally between a receptionist job, her burgeoning modelling career, and partying. Always partying. Mum and Dad had a shared interest in doing coke and dancing to disco, and six weeks into seeing each other romantically, they ran off to Jamaica to get married. On a dare. Literally. One of their friends dared them to get married, and the two cokeheads actually took that dare, almost certainly unaware that this last frivolous bit of 1970s chutzpah would yield two children and seventeen years of unhappy marriage. But they took the dare and fucked off to Montego Bay to be married in shotgun fashion by Percival Lancelot, Esq., justice of the peace and blacksmith. And so, as newlywed disco kids, undoubtedly fucked up on liquor, coke, Quaaludes, and God knows what else, Mum and Dad came back to Montreal, and everything would be different. They probably didn't notice it at first—the changes in each era are rarely noticed by those taking part in them—but that winter, as December turned into the 1980s, as the eras shifted, so did the paradigms for my mother, my father, and the Canadiens.

I was an accident. My parents have admitted as much and, considering their lifestyle at the time, this was to be expected. They were young and on drugs. Getting arrested in a one-bedroom full of cocaine, scales, baggies, and a 9mm with the serial number shaved off doesn't exactly reek of forethought. Mum became aware that she was carrying me sometime in the second half of 1981, and on that day she resolved to get clean. And that was it. Cold turkey. Because she was a mother now, and no rail of coke could match the import of what she was becoming. They were married and starting a family, and it was time to grow up, and the Habs got swept by the Oilers in the first round. For the rest of his life, Dad would have an on-again, off-again affair with legitimacy and going straight, but as mentioned, his first true love was drug life: dealing drugs and doing them. He would quit dealing them, but not before going away to prison for half a year following a raid on Mum and Dad's apartment by the Mounties. And as for doing drugs, well, he would never quit that.

When he got out of prison, my old man took to corporate life like the proverbial fish to water. The Western world was in the process of getting over its last bit of residual Woodstock guilt and shamelessly allowing itself to enjoy the slick monetary excesses of the "Me Decade." At least, that would be the vibe in the transition montage of the made-for-TV movie of Dad's life, though I'm still not sure who would play him; the famous person that Dad most resembled was Saddam Hussein, but Saddam Hussein's acting career never really took off. The point is, aggressive capitalism was fetishized almost as much as materialism itself, and coke was still cool. All of this suited my father, the street-corner hustler and hazzer from Ville Saint-Laurent, to a T. He loved moving product and was now just moving product of a different variety. Cocaine and weed turned to semiconductors and microchips as he became a sales rep for a computer electronics distribution company. Hustling was hustling, and he was good at it. Plus, he always liked wearing suits. Money rolled in and Dad took every opportunity to enjoy the fruits of joining the rat race: golf clubs and country clubs, Pierre Cardin socks, state-of-the-art hi-fi, a sweet car. And then there were the perks.

The company Dad worked for had season tickets to the Forum, and one might assume this would have just been fucking Valhalla for a truly devout and lifelong Habs fan. And it was, just not necessarily in the way one might think.

In the 1980s, the Canadiens were fighting an uphill battle in an evolving league. Waves of expansion and the ensuing thinning of the draft pool saw the Habs' position as standard-bearer of the NHL and spiritual home of the Stanley Cup sincerely challenged and threatened for the first time in the team's history. This would be a taste of things to come. The Habs would make multiple trips to the playoffs, but would usually find a way to get stymied. Twice by the fucking Nordiques.

And then along came Patrick. In 1985/86, a band of plucky underdogs, backed by a hotheaded Québécois goaltending phenom, found a way to turn what was basically a .500 season into a string of crazy overtime wins that ultimately saw the Cup come back to Montreal for the first time in seven years. Patrick Roy would, of course, go on to be crucified by Habs fandom, and then be traded away to the reanimated corpse of the Nordiques, the Colorado Avalanche, for no defensible reason. And then the whole shitty passion play would happen all over again, twenty years later, with P.K. Subban.

But more on that later. Before Roy left to win two Stanley Cups with Colorado, he won two Stanley Cups with

Montreal. All of a sudden there was a mostly new roster of legends to be carved onto the Cup for time immemorial, and my father worked at a place that had season tickets to their stadium.

Having access to free and readily available tickets to the most hallowed building in the history of hockey was the stuff of a lifetime's worth of dreams for every kid from Montreal. And Dad was no exception. But as with most things of sincere personal significance, Dad had something of a contradictory relationship with the Canadiens. He loved them dearly, just as he loved my sister and me, and Mum. But it was *his* love, on his conditions, and his shit would always take priority. And when he actually achieved said access, Dad didn't always use it to see the Habs, up close and personal, any more than he'd ever done in his life. No, he would use the hookup to go down to the Forum in his suit and tie and fucking scalp the tickets. He would tell his boss something along the lines of "I want to take my kid [me] to see the Habs. Can I get the tickets for tonight?" His boss would oblige, and Dad would hop in his car and head down to Atwater, no doubt filled with the unique satisfaction that comes from feeling you've pulled one over on someone. One time, Dad went to scalp at the Forum whilst sporting a cast on his right hand, broken while playing hockey drunk on beer and stoned on whatever the fuck. Some scalper, being a member of what I imagine are a territorial group of people, took exception to Dad selling tickets on his turf. Dad punched his cast-covered right into the scalper's face, hopped in the car, and came home to watch the game.

He rarely missed one. Whether watching on TV or listening on the radio, in French or in English, Dad really did follow and love that team. He just loved them in his own fucked-up way, same as he did us.

I distinctly remember waking up on my fifth birthday to find a padded manila envelope addressed to me, on Montreal Canadiens letterhead. Inside was a signed letter from Bob Gainey and glossy black-and-white 8x10s signed by the entire 1986/87 Montreal Canadiens team, including Patrick Roy, Chris Chelios, and Larry Robinson, to name a few. Sadly, this was lost on me at the time, as it had nothing to do with Transformers, G.I. Joe, or anything space related. Space was the theme of that year's party, complete with aluminum foil costumes and a green food-coloured orange juice/apple juice hybrid that my mother dubbed "moon juice." Obviously I would grow to appreciate how fucking crazy a gift it is to have autographs of the entirety of that year's Habs team, and it has only become more important and valuable over time. Dad got that for me. Somehow.

He was always doing that—pulling out random and amazing presents and experiences that none of us had any business having. The year *Batman* came out, those toys were absolutely impossible to find anywhere. Like the Power Rangers or Beanie Babies or Pokémons to come, the official Batman action figures and vehicles were the Holy Grail of Christmas presents for every red-blooded Canadian boy in 1989. I had long accepted that Santa probably wasn't going to be able to find many, if any, of the Batman toys I had on my list. I was very aware of how elusive these toys were and that we were not a wealthy family. But lo and behold, Christmas morning came and I galloped downstairs to find every Batman toy under the tree! Well, almost every. Everything but Bob the Goon, so whatever. Batman, the Joker, the Batcave, the Bat-mobile, the Batwing—fucking all of it was there! My mind was blown clear out of my skull. Years later, I would find out that Dad had called in a favour, or possibly asked a new one, from an associate of his from the old days who was now working as an executive at the company that manufactured the Batman toys. There was always some sort of hookup to be had, and it would often result in me getting something fucking insane that still boggles my mind to this day.

This was my father. He was also the man who would drive our entire family everywhere, high and drunk and speeding like a motherfucker. My father got into car crashes the way most people change a Brita filter. He was just always fucked up. From 11 a.m. on, every day, he was a very high-functioning alcoholic and drug addict, and this was just normal life for him. He had no qualms about taking me with him when meeting up with his dealer. I have fairly vivid memories of multiple visits to see Dad's friend, a fifty- or sixty-year-old Jamaican guy with grey dreads sitting in a barber's chair being waited on by multiple women. He was always super-nice to me and would give me a lollipop or something, and I'd go sit and look at magazines while he and Dad would do their thing. None of that struck Dad as odd. He was proving that he could live his life by his rules; he could combine and blend all of it and pull it off. Dad loved us, yes, but in his way, on his terms, and ultimately it wasn't enough.

The old man tried to teach me, but a lot of it didn't take. I couldn't care less about throwing or catching a baseball, and I was never all that fussed about being able to skate. There are two things, however, Dad taught me that have profoundly affected me and are a huge part of who I am today. He taught me to be proud, and he taught me to go through a brick wall for those I care about. I was never scared as a kid because I always knew Dad would rip a guy's head off if anyone ever fucked with us. He also taught me to stand up for myself and to walk tall and not be cowed by bullies.

My sister, Taylor, was born in October 1987, and six months later we moved to Oshawa, Ontario. We would move back to Montreal in the winter of 1993. This brief but formative sojourn in the heart of Leafs Nation explains not only my strange nasal twang, but also part of why my Habs fandom is as strong as it is. For five years, I wore the only Habs toque at a school full of Leafs toques, and no amount of teasing or ostracizing made me even consider denying my "Montrealness." Not that I had a choice. The Habs were the only team that was ever on TV in our house, and everything in my room was wall-to-wall Bleu Blanc Rouge. Yes, even my hamper. The point is, I was raised to be proud of who I was and where I was from, and five years in enemy territory only emboldened us.

This is the best of my father's legacy in me. The Oshawa years would be the beginning of the end for my dad and for the Habs as we knew them. There would be one more Stanley

Cup and one more go at being a family. But for Habs fans and Clan Baruchel, it was becoming clear that shit was different and the worst was yet to come. We did our very best impression of a suburban nuclear family, but regardless of what you may have heard, Oshawa is not some sort of lovers' paradise, a panacea for marital ills, the Paris of the Durham region. No, it's none of those things, and if there are cracks in a marriage's surface, it seems that five and a half years of exile in a place you're at odds with—which my mother very much was from the word go—living with a man you're at odds with, will only serve to exacerbate them. Still, we soldiered on. Or, at least, Mum soldiered on. Taylor and I were just children, and Mum went out of her way to shield us from whatever emotional and financial problems were plaguing her marriage.

For me, it was a time of toys and comics and movies, and playing two years of softball for Cedar Ridge, one of them under the powder-keg leadership of Serge Baruchel, manager and general firebrand. I was awful at the game, save for my ability to bodycheck the ball out of the gloves of basemen as I sloppily slid into first. It didn't happen often; I found a way to pull it off maybe three times, but, holy fuck, each time I did? My version of *The Goonies*! But really, I was garbage at softball just like I was—and am!—garbage at most sports. That being said, a lot of my friends from school or Beavers were on that team, and I really enjoyed the whole bench vibe: drinking Gatorade, adjusting jock straps, and doing *Wayne's World* impressions. We were a good team as well, having made it to the city-wide semifinals at the end of both seasons, only to be knocked out by each of our two dreaded regular-season rivals, Nipigon Park and Connaught. Those teams always had our number; whether during the regular season or at the championships, our games were always particularly tense affairs, for kids and grown-ups alike.

The Habs more or less floundered for the first few years of the decade, and the Bruins found a way to knock us out of the playoffs not once but three fucking times in a row. Three times in a row those scoundrels and motherfuckers sent us golfing. And then, in 1993, thanks to Montreal being Montreal, Habs fans began to entertain a conversation that would have been totally unthinkable just two years prior: Should we trade Patrick Roy? But thanks to rock-solid defending anchored by Habs fandom's favourite mercurial goaltender/pariah/martyr, and a remarkably potent offence led by the scoring efforts of no less than four different players who made it past the thirty-goal mark, and despite a panic-inducing end-of-season tailspin in which they would win only eight of their final nineteen games, the Canadiens skidded into the playoffs and onto their twenty-fourth and most recent, if not to say final, Stanley Cup. On the way there, they would record ten different playoff overtime victories, an all-time record that stands to this day. Also, Patrick Roy winked at Wayne Gretzky.

It was magical, and that summer the old man was just ebullient. We peeled around the Rice Lake region, my dad gunning the fuck out of our 1987 Cutlass Cruiser station wagon, "Old Betsy," smashing his fist on the horn in rhythmic succession, singing *"Les Canadiens sont là!"* at the top of his phlegmy lungs.

I remember Dad, drunk as shit and full of beans, metaphorical and actual. Though he might not actually have eaten beans that night. He ate beans, but I can't say, definitively: "Dad ate beans on whatever night that was when we were up at a cottage we rented." He probably just ate hamburgers or something. Anyway, Dad stuck a stick into our little bonfire until the tip was a glowing ember, pulled it out, and started drunkenly waving it about, writing *"Les champions de la Coupe Stanley!"* in the night air. That this is what he wrote I can confirm with complete accuracy, as his fire-writing was accompanied by narration. And when I say "narration," I mean Dad was bellowing the words out into the air and laughing. I loved it and believed this to be a very entertaining and hilarious bit of theatre. Taylor was six, so this sort of thing was right up her alley too. I honestly can't remember my mother's reaction. Dad was having a blast. His team were champions, he was at the cottage with his wife and son and daughter, and he was high and drunk as fuck.

In the TV movie in which Saddam Hussein plays my father, this scene would end with a fade to black. Saddam-as-Serge's voice echoes in the dark for a few beats before petering out to nothing. Then we smash cut to December 2, 1995. SadDad sits on the couch beside Mum—played by . . . Deborah Harry?—and watches, aghast, as Patrick Roy plays his last game for the Montreal Canadiens and gives his team the middle finger on national television. DadDam turns to BlondieMum and says: "We'll never win another Stanley Cup again." We cut to a close-up of the TV screen and watch in slow motion as Patrick Roy walks down the tunnel and away forever.

We then leap ahead three years to see our moustachioed anti-hero sitting on the couch, alone, in a sparsely decorated one-bedroom apartment. He watches the Habs on a small television. His family is nowhere to be seen. He picks up the phone and dials a number. The phone rings and rings and rings. Finally, Dad hangs up. No one wants to speak to him.

Now, obviously, I've left a bunch of stuff out. It's all very sad stuff, and I was already in bed with this Saddam bit. Plus, I've probably already exhausted a good deal of my "being earnest" capital in this one chapter.

Needless to say, my mother eventually divorced my father and he moved out. Equally needless to say is the fact that my father did not take this well. This bit of trauma and transition did not cure him of his disease; quite the opposite—he only got more fucked up. By the end, he would be damned well close to penniless and living off his girlfriend, Linda. He was also buying handguns and picking fights on Crescent Street and suffering from the pain of having a son who refused to have any contact with him. He faded away and finally OD'd in 2004, at the age of forty-nine. He would leave behind a great deal of debt in child support owed to my sister and to me, as well as a legacy that is as contradictory to itself as it is fundamental to my everyday life.

The Habs would keep finding new nadirs to descend to, culminating in what remains the worst record in franchise history.

Looking back now, it's hard for me not to juxtapose the image of my father in the last days of his life, kicking about the video-poker-machine-ridden coke bars of NDG, against the image of my father in the seventies, in the prime of his life, conquering the world and everything in it. It's equally hard not to juxtapose the image of the Habs at the end of the nineties—or the dawn of the aughts, or the dawn of the teens, for that matter—hopelessly middling and suffocated by history, against the Habs of the seventies, electric and iconic and afraid of no one.

Obviously I wasn't there, but I've heard Dad's stories and seen the albums' worth of his photos and listened to the records that filled his steamer trunk. I've read the stats and seen the documentaries and watched the tapes of old games. I know that era's version of my dad like I know that era's version of the Habs. I know them both in a romantic, origin-story sort of way. Titans of a golden age long passed, doers of legendary deeds to be referenced for all time. To know and understand the Habs now is to study who they were then. Just as to know and understand my dad now is to try to get who Serge was then.

Then, when everything was victory and rebellion and everyone was immortal and no one had any idea what the future would be. I know my father then.

I know that, even if he knew exactly how and where he'd end up, standing there in the middle of the seventies he wouldn't change a fucking thing.

WE ARE STILL YOUNG

We are still young
Not still,
But young
There is time still
For us to burn our
Victories
Time still for us
To make Iron our defeats
And scream on heaven
"We are still young"
Not still, but young
There is time still
Time for us
Still

00:20:00

SECOND PERIOD

AND IT CONTINUES. Our smoke break ends, and we come back inside. The smell of our bad habit is somehow both compounded and mitigated by Manitoba's sub-zero winter air, or by the dryness of the California night. I am at the Air Canada Centre, or the Staples Center, or I am in a short-term rental apartment in Winnipeg or at my friend's condo in LA or at a sports bar in Toronto. I am not home. I am away. And I know, without having to check the time, that the intermission is almost done. I know that once this car/beer/antidepressant/yogurt/male shower product's commercial finally shuts up and cuts to black, the Habs will file out of the visitor's tunnel and onto a fresh sheet of ice, in a building foreign and unfriendly. This is someone else's barn.

We went into the break a goal down, but this is a different period. The Zamboni has polished away most evidence of the previous stanza's narrative. That cleansing, coupled with a twenty-minute reset full of all sorts of potential second winds and coming to of senses, always makes the second period feel almost like the start of a whole new story. Especially when you're down a goal. But it isn't the start of a new story; it's the continuation of the one that started an hour ago, but really four months ago. It's the middle of the season, and it's February, and it's garbage outside, and the prospects for the remainder of our season seem to dovetail with our chances at winning this game. Could really go either way, with defeat more likely than victory. Same as it ever was.

Our jackets and/or sweaters come off as our boots are kicked free of snow, or sneakers are removed out of respect for someone else's carpet, the secret hope that LA hasn't made my feet smell like cheese covered in cat shit never far from my mind. Obviously, I don't take my shoes off in a sports bar, because that would be super-gross and would likely bar me from being served food and beverages. I order way more appetizers in a sports bar than I do in any other restaurant. Anyway, the point is, I settle back down onto a chair, or a couch I don't own, and my attention is once again trained on the TV screen.

I am away, but I am still with friends. Some of them are Habs fans, expats away from home. Others are from elsewhere. Sometimes, but not often—especially when I'm in Los Angeles, a city of entertainment industry transplants—they are from whatever city I am currently visiting. They are all friends of mine, some closer than others. Their hometown or status as Habs fans in no way guarantees them being closer with me than others. I've watched many a Habs game with people I'd describe as acquaintances at best. That being said, there is something of a shorthand or familiarity amongst expats that can never be recreated outside the community. There is something special about being at home while being away.

That's how it feels at my buddy Ricky's place. We've known each other since I was twelve and he was eleven, and the bulk of any trip to LA is spent in the confines of the Anglo Montreal embassy that is the two-bedroom he's shared with his lady, Cierra, for most of a decade. Ricky is basically Opie from *The Andy Griffith Show* all grown up. And he usually does an impression of his mother. When I am here, there is no edge whatsoever. Not even a subtle one, which is usually the case for me when I am out and about, and particularly when I am far from home. There is a slight tension, an almost covert anxiety that permeates everything outside my comfort zone. I have anxiety disorder, and that is simply the cost of being a functioning member of society. So it's especially appreciated that I can literally cross the continent and find myself in a cozy apartment, surrounded by people I love and things I recognize. Like the Habs. One minute I am in a city where I have never felt at home, at odds with everything from the traffic to the sun, and the next I am nestled into the couch, watching TSN or RDS on a TV in Hollywood, and I am instantly that much more comfortable. Ricky is a lifelong hockey lover and Habs fan, and if I'm watching the Habs in LA, chances are I'm with him.

Or I'm at the Staples Center, decked out in Bleu Blanc Rouge, proudly representing my home and, sometimes deliberately, antagonizing the locals. We have two options when faced with stuff that makes us nervous: fight or flight. My instincts have almost always screamed the second thing, except when it comes to pride in where I'm from. I am as susceptible to all the old tribal buttons as anyone, and there is something that comes out of me, some weird bit of courage, when I am in enemy territory. It's not confidence so much as it is aggression. At home I am confident because I am surrounded by other members of my tribe. Away, I feel aggressive because we are outnumbered, the berserker bravery of the cornered animal palpable in even the slightest form. I scream and boo and cheer just as loudly away as I do at home. I rep my team, surrounded by thousands of people repping another, and I am not the least bit timid because of it. If anything, I am that much more emboldened by the status quo of edge while away.

I don't want to make it seem like I go around picking fights or talking shit, because I don't. Usually. That doesn't change the fact that there is *always* someone who takes issue with our presence. Especially in the States.

There are three times in my adult life where I was legitimately close to getting into a fist fight, and two of them were at hockey games in California. I'm not going to blow any minds by saying that Americans are very patriotic as a rule, but I will say that they certainly seem to get way more upset at other people being psyched about their respective countries than any other nationality I've encountered. This is not to say that there aren't nationalistic or xenophobic assholes in other countries, nor is it to say that all Americans are nationalistic or xenophobic. I'm saying that every time I watch the Habs play the Kings in California, someone gets mad or annoyed at me for cheering for my team. They take it personally. Obviously, the Bell Centre isn't the fucking Ritz for people in Bruins jerseys, but we don't seem to give nearly as much of a shit when there's like one dude wearing a Kings hat standing up after Jarret Stoll did something. In the Staples Center, I get a lot of cross looks and people turning around to give me a piece of their mind and ask me pointed, rhetorical questions like "What country are you in right now?"

Which is verbatim what a lady said to me after overhearing me ask a kid in a Kings jersey "How many Olympic gold medals does Jonathan Quick have?" which was, itself, a direct reply to him asking me "How many Stanley Cup rings does Carey Price have?" My raising of the stakes from NHL to Olympic standards was apparently egregious enough of an attack on George Washington and McDonald's and *Full House* that the lady in front of me felt the patriotic urge to try to subordinate me. I remember asking her what that had to do with anything, which I think yielded a "Well, I like Jonathan Quick" before she turned back to watch the game and, I assume, felt weird with me sitting behind her. I know I always feel weird when I argue with a stranger and then neither of us leave and they're behind me and I just have to pretend that I'm enjoying the game or movie and am not obsessed with nightmare scenarios of all the potential weird hijinks happening back there. Are they aiming a gun at my head? Who knows? Should I have been shit-talking with a thirteen-year-old kid to begin with? Probably not, but also who knows?

Americans seem to take issue with the very idea that we'd have the temerity to be as loud as they are in their own house, and the teams are quickly turned into analogues for the two countries. Everything is filtered through that, and before I know it, "Habs suck" or "Fuck the Habs" is replaced by "Go back to Canada" or "Fuck Canada" or "Get in your fucking car," and now I'm standing in a parking lot in Anaheim, trying to decide which of the four white-trash dudes from Orange County I'm going to have to punch first. I have it narrowed down to the two biggest guys. One is a tall, fat guy I've some-how managed to nickname "Lumpy" at some point during the two minutes of our interaction. The other is a short, stocky guy who works out a lot and is wearing a T-shirt that says OLD NAVY on it. Even though the stocky guy is the one who told me to get in my fucking car, I settle on Lumpy, since he is technically the biggest and I think if I punch him in the throat, the others will get scared. I'm also wondering why none of the four people I came here with have gotten out of the car yet. The Habs got their asses kicked in a stadium filled with people making duck sounds, and a lot of them have been giving us a lot of shit from the moment we arrived. We got a "Fuck Can-ada" within two minutes of showing up, and that about sums up the tenor of our interactions with the people of Anaheim that night.

Eventually, my buddy Walker would notice I was about to fight four people and quickly leap to the fore; as he is a man who once stomped a biker's head in a bar fight, this was all much more his kind of thing than it was mine. Pretty soon, the stocky guy was back to his "Get back in your fucking car" routine, only this time directed at Walker, to which he replied, "You talk a lot of shit, Old Navy." And then they were nose to nose, and then Walker's girlfriend, Jess, and their friend were in the dudes' faces, saying, "This is why your country is going to get bombed," and I'm not quite sure how the fuck he did it, but all of a sudden there was Walker, bro-hugging Old Navy, saying something about "At the end of the day, we're all on the same side." Which I think was something to do with Afghanistan. I'm not sure, but it worked, and we all got in our cars and split. It was all very preposterous.

Equally preposterous was getting into it in the washroom of the Staples Center with some drunk middle-aged guy on a cellphone who had tried to cut in front of me and then, when he couldn't, accused me of doing the same thing to him. I remember yelling, "You're going to pee. I'm going to pee. Everybody's going to pee!" and some guy at a urinal saying, "I guess he didn't know you wrote *Goon*," which garnered a laugh from a few other bathroom dudes. It was the most pride I have ever felt in a room full of strangers pissing.

At Ricky's place, settling back down onto the couch, I crunch up some more weed. Most of it will go into a joint; the leftovers are packed into the bowl of a bong, and I take a big rip. The commercial ends and we get a brief flurry of stats from other games being played tonight. Ricky says, "Well, Chris my Kunitz!" as I cough a lot and the second period begins. Whatever we had for supper has been replaced by bags of gummy candy, ice cream sandwiches, cookies, or Canadian chocolate bars smuggled Stateside with care. I mean, not actually smuggled. They literally sell them at the airport. The care is real, though. And so is the eating of junk food. And the eighteen fillings I have. And counting. Also, like four root canals. And one of my two front guys is false. My teeth are garbage. And not because I inherited bad dental genes or something, or had a butch sports injury. I literally just ate a bunch of sugar for two decades. Even the front tooth got knocked out from doing something lame. No, it wasn't from hockey or a bar fight or too radical of an ollie on my skateboard or whatever. It was from a fucking rhythm exercise in drama class. Anyway, fuck my teeth.

The second begins with a whimper, the intensity of the first replaced by its pale cousin. The boys look sluggish, like there was no intermission at all. There is no discernible rhythm, as play is whistled dead twice in the first minute. The team looks frantic, and yet somehow they're still too slow. Whatever potential reset there might have been has been thoroughly nullified, and now this is not a whole new period but a continuation of the previous. We are down a goal, and on the back foot, and grappling for consistency. There are others in the room. I can't say they're watching the game like we are. They are here to hang out and smoke weed, and eventually watch fails or play video games. They're just here for a visit, and the game will never mean as much to them as it does to us. They check their phones and bide their time until the next joint or smoke exodus or whatever bit of tonight's visit they can actually connect to. They are apathetic about the game at hand, and I can't blame them. Soon their apathy becomes contagious and we're checking phones too.

And then, as is the way in hockey, comes something vivid that stirs the blood. Seemingly out of nowhere, moribund routine transforms into a flourish, a moment of inspiration that galvanizes the senses. In this case, it's a big, open-ice hit. One of our guys fucking obliterates one of theirs, pretty much smack dab at centre ice. The words "Holy fuck" leave my mouth almost instantaneously. The room's attention is now on the TV; no one is checking their phone. Even if they don't like the Habs, even if they don't understand hockey, they understand what they just saw. It was simple, and pure, and profound. "Jeezus . . ." I mutter as they show replay after replay of our guy drilling the other guy into oblivion. We are not a physical team, and we're usually on the receiving end of this shit, so it's always doubly impactful on the rare occasion it happens. The other guy is only now getting to his feet, his bell fucking rung as shit. Ricky does his Mum voice: "My heavens . . ." The other team takes issue with our hit, which was chintzy at best. When it comes to plays that skirt the edge, that could go either way, judgement-wise, I naturally frame our shit in the most positive light. My bias doesn't really allow for chintzy hits, only clean ones and then fucking super-dirty ones where I have no choice but to say, "Yeah, that was right on the numbers. That's fucked." This time, however, I am convinced that any head contact was incidental, that our guy was just playing hockey.

The home team doesn't think so, and in an instant, all of their skaters are on all of our skaters. Before long, the scrum of angry men is concentrated down to two champions who will let God dictate how clean the hit was by the ancient rite of the duel. Some years the Habs have a guy who knows how to throw and take a punch. Others we are just simply outclassed, size-wise, from the word go, and though we might have guys who are fearless or courageous, we know they will be punching above their weight no matter what. More often than not, we have a bunch of guys who could go either way, depending on a bunch of factors, not the least of which is the other guy. This is one of those years, and as one of our guys drops his gloves and throws up his dukes, his actions mirrored by their guy, I already know it's not going to go well. I can tell the other guy wants it more, just as I can tell he does this more often than our guy does. Even if fighting is all but dead in the NHL, it still happens in a lot of the leagues these players are sourced from. There are still men who do this for a living, and as each old-fashioned one-on-one bout becomes more of a novelty and less the status quo, the violence gap will only widen.

Our guy and their guy grab a hold of one another and tussle for a bit, jockeying for advantage. Our guy is very much outmuscled by his opponent, who looks as if he's merely figuring our guy out, like a mover divining the best way to pick up a particularly cumbersome fridge. And then it happens: the other guy gets one hand free and starts raining punches down on our guy. Our guy eats way more of them than he should before he throws his arms around the other guy in a last-ditch effort to stop the onslaught. The two players grapple for a few more seconds before the other guy puts our guy on his ass and the refs skate in to officially break up the fight and ensure it stays broken up. The other guy is cheered on by his crowd, their champion having bested ours. Their city that much prouder than ours. The Habs bang their sticks on the boards in a show of respect for our guy, who just did a job none of them have any interest in doing. The players skate to their respective boxes, and I turn away from the screen for the first time in a bit. Ricky and I exchange cringes, and I sigh. "Oy vey." We both shake our heads, and then launch into a shared tirade about how small we are, how nobody is intimidated by our blue line.

Our tirade quickly shifts into a back and forth about various fights we remember watching where our guy won. Eventually, our talk becomes an anachronistic lament festival, and we are both longing for eras that neither of us lived through. Because we are Habs fans and every victory seems behind us. Logic would dictate us being calloused by such institutional cynicism, and yet every loss sucks just as bad. And there are many different ways to lose. You can lose a game. You can tank a season. You can shit the bed when it matters most. Those are the big, bold, obvious ones. Then there is a whole panoply of frustration-inducing paper cuts that the true fan suffers. Every blown lead, every turnover, every selfish failed pirouette, every punch eaten, every heroic stride forward that should have been a conservative stride back, every unselfish waste of time that is often just panic; all of it stings. All of it reminds us of where our team is in the history book of the Habs.

We are still in the throes of feeling sorry for ourselves when our attention is forced back to the TV as the Habs allow another goal. My "For fuck's sake" comes out about two seconds behind Ricky's "Fuck!" Frustration has turned to anger has turned to ruefulness. This is the bit where we pretend to flirt with giving up. "Goddammit," I continue, as I get up to pace. As if me being on my feet might somehow affect what the fuck is happening in a stadium thousands of miles away. We watch replays of the goal and try to discern how soft it was. Even if it was, we won't belabour the point, because our goalie is only human. And he works his ass off. And he is almost always the standout or sole bright spot on this team. Whatever surname might be stitched on the back of his sweater, it is a natural law of the Habs that the goalie will most likely be the best player on our team. It has been this way for the duration of my life. We overachieve on the backs of goalies the way the Leafs overpay thirty-eight-year-olds. In this case, the goal wasn't soft, and he's faced almost twice as many shots as his counterpart. It's rarely our goalie's fault. It's almost always that our skaters have hung him out to dry.

The second period is drawing to a close, we are two goals

down, and one of our guys got his ass kicked. It is midway through the season, and nothing about this is fun. All of a sudden, the year feels longer, the game more tedious. We start questioning why we need eighty-two games in the regular season. This is when it feels like the Habs are only ever in half-empty American stadiums and I am constantly falling asleep. These are the ides of hockey.

I'm already on my way outside for the next smoke break, my interest in the final seconds of this period well and truly waned, when, of course, we score. Because we're the Habs, and we are always a random bit of finesse away from being dangerous. Instantly, the jaded old barfly in me, the crabby old bugger who pre-emptively judges his team as a self-defence mechanism, is replaced by a child. We cheer, and I pogo towards the TV. My mouth agape, my adrenaline coursing, I plant myself back down on the couch, saying something like "Ohhhh" as I watch replays of our guy dangling in on net, feinting before going top shelf with a backhander. It is filthy, and beautiful, and this is what we do when we are at our best. We have no consistency, and we're small as fuck, but something seems to happen when a player puts on our sweater. Any player seems capable of individual, highlight-reel inspiration when they're a Hab. Now, this means fuck all when you're talking about winning whole seasons and, ideally, challenging for the Cup. But when you're down in the nitty-gritty of a game, when all that's in front of you are all the little ways to lose and win, these are the moments that lift you up or, God help you, get you back in the game.

Which is where I'm at. It was a lovely goal, and regardless of what my brain is telling me, my heart knows we are still in this fight.

There's a lot of hockey left to be played.

From: JB [jay@fakeemailforthepurposesofthisconceit.com]
Sent: Tuesday, January 29, 2018, 16:57 PM
To: Bruins, The Boston <bruins@nhl.com>
Subject: I hate you

Hi there, Bruins.

I hate you. As I am a Habs fan, true and true, I'm sure you wouldn't have it any other way. But yes, I fucking hate you.

I come by my hate honestly, as I was raised in a house where your logo, and your sweater, were about as welcome as Lyme disease. Or Don Cherry's opinions. Or Leafs merchandise. Even the Leafs didn't garner the kind of visceral rage that you guys do. Don't get me wrong, we always hated the Leafs too, but we kind of just rolled our eyes at them. And shook our heads at Quebec. But Boston? Boston we raised our fists at. We fucking hate(d) Boston.

It's the particular brand of rock-solid hatred that vulcanizes over a lifetime of facing an adversary you truly respect, or maybe even fear. Yeah, fine, I said it. There's a respect. And maybe a bit of fear. Because you're the "Big, Bad Bruins" and there seems to be a long-cherished New England pastime of sending Habs to the hospital. Even my mum, rarely one to give any kind of shit about any kind of sport, would adopt a disenfranchised wince whenever she'd talk about Boston. She probably couldn't tell you what team Sidney Crosby plays for, but she could tell you that she hates the Bruins.

First off, I hate you because I hate Boston, because that's what people from Montreal do, just as I know a great many of you humble folk come up to our town to get drunk and treat it like an ashtray and be racist and dry-hump women. Obviously this is not everybody from Boston—it probably isn't even most— but it's like at least half. Even if it's less, the point is, I hate you because we hate you and you hate us. Just as you hate on our accent and French signs everywhere and the fact that we don't shoot each other as often as you do, we hate on your accent and Abercrombie hoodies and the fact that you're always picking fights and shit-talking everything the whole time. And your accent. Yes, I know I already mentioned it, but really, your accent is fucked. I've got friends in and from Boston, and they're chill as fuck, but the vast majority of their neighbours that make the trip up aren't the greatest ambassadors for the city. Up here, that accent is most commonly heard used by "people" getting kicked out of bars or drunk-chanting "U-S-A" or arguing with someone in the service industry. And shit-talking everything the whole time. Take whatever white-trash pride you will from the fact that during all the time I had season tickets to the Bell Centre, the only times I ever saw police barricades or fist fights in the stands was when the Bruins were in town.

I hate you because you're the bad guys. Yes, I'm a Habs fan, so there's most of it right there, but I believe it goes beyond moral relativism. You guys really seem to like being villains. Some seventies-era sportswriter with a penchant for alliteration, and probably some sort of buzz on, called you the "Big, Bad Bruins," and you've just leaned into it like a motherfucker. You look like the bad guys from a fucking movie—like the huge, evil, overfunded team that Rob Lowe, Paul Newman, and the Mighty

Ducks have to best in the third act. Even your name is more evil than it had to be. You weren't content with the affront to civilization and God that is naming yourselves after mankind's immortal enemy, the bear; like an institutional tribute to ursine mysticism and totalitarianism, you had to choose as arcane a word for *bear* as possible. You pissed on the graves of the thousands if not millions of human beings who have been killed by bears. Also, like any truly scary movie villain, your outfits are literally black. And yellow. As if you were faced with a dizzying spectrum of heraldic and symbolic possibilities and went, "Fuck, yeah, I want to play in the ancient international colours of evil and moral cowardice." You're bear worshippers. Evil, cowardly, godless bear worshippers.

Also, you actually look like movie villains. From Derek Sanderson through Cam Neely on to Milan Lucic or Brad Marchand, you've bent over backwards to ensure that your team is constantly populated by the most detestable on-ice heels, fiends, and blackguards in the league. Nobody looks at Brad Marchand and goes, "He'd make a great Batman." And there's the same heroism deficit with Lucic, whose Pleistocene perma-scowl inspires few and weirds out many. Marchand could probably be the Riddler, though. Maybe Lucic could be Bane. The point is, the Bruins always seem to pick the scary guys. In no player is this more evident than in Slovakian Bond henchman/grain elevator/ Grendel Zdeno Chara, whose ability to intimidate and horrify is matched only by his Galactus-like ability to devour whole planets. He was a scary man before he hit Max Pacioretty into a stanchion, thus breaking a vertebrae in his neck, and a generational monster after. Like the boss at the end of a video game level, or the big bad at the end of a movie, Chara is the living, breathing embodiment of all the Bruins evil that the Habs must defeat if we are to succeed.

And in the playoffs, somehow, it always seems to end up like that. Us against you. If it's late spring and we're still playing hockey, chances are we will play it against you at some point. No two teams have faced each other more. One hundred and seventy-seven games through thirty-four different post-season series, to be specific. Like Batman and the Joker, facing each other again and again, across myriad reboots, remakes, and multiverses, the Habs and the Bruins have been fighting this fight since long before I was born, and they will be fighting this fight long after I'm gone. And just as Batman does with the Joker, we've got your number, victory-wise. Historically, anyway. For throughout history, time and time again, defying odds and expectations, we have found a way to win the vast majority of those games. One hundred and six individual games and twenty-five series, to be specific.

But you already knew that. Of course you did, because as stereotypically big and bad as you are, you are, in fact, scared of us. We are your villains by virtue of us having kicked the shit out of you way more times than you've kicked the shit out of us. Like the times in *Star Trek* where you jump into the Klingon point of view and understand how weird and evil Star Fleet seems to them, if I put myself in your shoes (or whatever Klingons wear on their feet), I can understand how fucking infuriating we must be. To have constantly had us, in all of our European flamboyance, on the ropes countless times, only to have us clench victory from the jaws of defeat more often than not, to have worked your asses off all season, to be within striking distance of what's rightfully yours, only to have it all taken away at the last minute by a bunch of figure-skating disco pussies, must be what it is to be driven insane. I get it. I'd hate us too. I mean, obviously, I already do hate us. But that's besides the point. This isn't about me. This is about you and why I hate you.

Okay, maybe this is about me, and how the reason I hate you as vehemently as I do is because I know the Habs aren't the Habs without the Bruins. Obviously the Leafs are important to us too, blah blah blah, but with you guys, our white-hot hatred is the real deal. Ours is the kind of hate people write and fight and riot about. Ours is the kind of hate that marketing executives salivate over and seek to synthetically recreate. Ours is the kind of hate that rides that thinnest of lines, love and respect only inches away. Because what the fuck is the point if not to root for the good guys and against the bad guys? I hate you because other teams are just places and nouns, whereas yours is the name of dread and evil and pagan bear worship on the lips of Habs fans everywhere. I hate you because I need to hate you, and I know this because I know that the Columbus Blue Jackets mean absolutely nothing to me. I hate you, and I know I'll hate you forever, and I take pride in knowing you'll hate me forever too.

I'll see you in hell.

JB

From: JB [jay@fakeemailforthepurposesofthisconceit.com]
Sent: Saturday, March 30, 2018, 23:42 PM
To: Maple Leafs, The Toronto <leafs@nhl.com>
Subject: I hate you

Dear Leafs,

I hate you.

I don't hate you in the all-consuming way I hate Boston or Quebec City. No, ours is something milder and closer. A tad more intimate. Almost forgiving. Like when you fucking hate your cousin or something. I hate you in that way, where I've no interest in hanging out with you, and everything about you annoys me, but at the end of the day, you're family and part of me has to love you. Even if almost none of me respects you. Allow me to elaborate.

The Leafs and Habs are born of the same land, have some shared heritage, and even share some individuals in common. Montreal and Toronto are the wellsprings of Confederation, and most of our prime ministers have claimed at least one of the two cities as their home. We have both been around a long-ass time, even though we both know that the Habs have been doing our thing longer than you guys. But the game itself, the game has been played on neighbourhood rinks pretty much since its inception. We might debate and argue over where exactly hockey was born, but we will both agree that it was *raised* in Montreal and Toronto, equally. And even though I believe Montreal is, in fact, hockey's true birthplace, I will readily admit that Toronto is hockey's capital, and has been for a long time.

Habs vs. Leafs is Canadian identity distilled down to its most binary and iconic. This was conflict that defined our nation long before the advent of television. Most of our country was one or the other, red or blue, from World War I well into the seventies. Habs vs. Leafs is an infinity of Canadian Saturday nights, and table hockey games, and completely different memories of generations' worth of shared moments. We are linked together forever in our opposition, and we have helped give voice to Canada in the process. This is why I can never truly hate you, because we have both served and moulded this country, and I pride myself on patriotism. Because I know and understand you and your context. Because we're related.

Not flip sides of the same coin, mind you, because there is precious little that we have in common. Thank fuck. But definitely related. Which means I can have a weird love for the Leafs whilst liking absolutely nothing about the Leafs whatsoever. Which is the case here. In fact, not only is there nothing I like about you, there is much I actively dislike about you.

Your name, for starters. It's not so much bad as it is dumb, because the plural of *leaf* is *leaves*. Now, obviously, I get that we're all in Canada, and the Maple Leaf, our national symbol, makes perfect sense in terms of fertile ground to mine a team name from. And I'm sympathetic to the conundrum you found yourselves in when it was time to reconcile committing to the Maple Leaf as your name with the fact that a hockey team has a bunch of people on it, and that North American sports team—naming convention usually dictates a pluralized noun following a place name. I am also sympathetic to the epiphany you guys must have had when you all went "Eureka!" and said, "Fuck it! Just write whatever!" And thus, the word *Leafs* was standardized, and accepted, and made official—a clever workaround and ruse, to be sure. And one you would probably have gotten away with, too, if not for the fact that English is one of Canada's two official languages and the mother tongue of the majority of Canadians. This in addition to the fact that English has generally been accepted as the lingua franca of the international business community for the last three hundred years or so. An unsightly, intentional typo like that doesn't go unnoticed.

Nor does the fact that, whilst naming yourselves after our national symbol, you don't play in red, as the leaf appears on our flag, nor have you played in the green of the leaf featured on our old flag, the Red Ensign, in a very long time. No, you picked the second most obvious thing in Canada to name a team after, second only to literally being called the Canadiens (yes, I know that's not what it means, fuck off), and then picked a colour combination of literally ZERO significance to the thing you're referencing. In fact, if anything, blue and white are the colours of Quebec's flag and the separatist movement in general, and thus not only unconnected to the Maple Leaf or Canada, but directly connected to arguably the world's only movement that could even kind of be called anti-Canadian. Morrissey and the seal hunt people are probably up there too. Anyway, your name is goofy as fuck. Which is fitting, because much about you is goofy as fuck.

I live in Toronto, and obviously I quite like it here, but make no mistake, Toronto is a huge nerd. I know this because I'm a huge nerd, and my nerd radar is top three in the world—not that nerds are usually hard to pick out. Or pick on. And even though I may be a nerd, my city isn't one. Montreal is many things—weird, snobby, cold, exasperating, infested with organized crime—but nerdy? No. Montreal isn't a nerd. If Montreal were a person, she'd be a forty-eight-year-old performance artist with a speed habit and a bunch of young boyfriends. If Toronto were a person, he'd be a WASPy ginger nerd who transcribes guitar tabs and plays a lot of new board games. Also, his haircuts would be more expensive than they are cool, and his parents would both be teachers from Wales, and he'd live to write negative Yelp! reviews. The point is, Toronto is a dork and Montreal isn't. And just as the Habs are an extension, an embodiment, of all that's angsty and rebellious in Montreal's very essence, the Leafs are an extension and embodiment of all that's Saxon and hospital food about Toronto's soul.

With the exception of the odd Mogilny, Antropov, or Kessel thrown in, the Leafs I've grown up hating have, for the most part, all been north or south of lunch pail or plumber. Wendel Clark, Tie Domi, Darcy Tucker, even Eric Lindros or Mats Sundin. All relatively quintessential versions of Don Cherry's hard-working, hard-nosed "Good Canadian Boy." These are the virtues your team holds aloft: doggedness, humility, and the Burkean ideal of truculence. And though the Oshawa in me understands much of it, the Montreal in me can't help but resist it. I suspect, even if we'd never moved back to Montreal, even if I'd stayed in Oshawa the rest of my life, it would still leave me wanting, or at least, it would never be a completely right fit. For although I am gentile as fuck on my mum's side, we are not WASPs. We are mackerel-eating, ashen-browed dock folk, and for better or worse, ours is an ancient tradition of colour, embellishment, and melodrama. Hard and tough, yes, but fiery and culturally articulate. The ethos and tenets of Leafism are commendable, but they don't scratch all my itches and ultimately seem boring and dorky.

Even your mascot is nerdy, relative to other mascots. Your mascot is an anthropomorphic polar bear named Carlton. Not that a big furry orange something or other named Youppi! is like miles ahead, cool-wise, but at least Youppi! has been around for a minute, having started life as the mascot for the Expos in the halcyon days of 1979 Montreal before dying, only to be resurrected as the mascot for the Habs. Just like Jesus. And just like Jesus, he has the stink of time, and experience, and vintage on him. Also like Jesus, one gets the feeling when one meets Youppi! that he would not have been out of place at Studio 54 in its heyday. Carlton the anthropomorphic polar bear looks like he'd be the first guy to get killed when a batch of new prisoners is dropped off at prison. Not Youppi! though. No, make no mistake, Youppi! will cut somebody's head off if he needs to. Like Jesus. And like Jesus, he was implicated in a suspected mob hit outside a mascot factory a few years back. None of this is true. The point is, fuck Carlton the Bear.

The Leafs are basically the exact opposite of everything I believe in or think is cool. Just as we, I assume, are the antithesis of everything you hold dear. Where we are extravagant and flamboyant, you are humble and folksy. Where we celebrate individual talent and showmanship, you lionize plumbers, and your owners or coaches or general managers are usually more famous than your players. (Consider the personality cults surrounding Brian Burke, Mike Babcock, or even MLSE itself. Not to mention the decades under the Ballard junta.) Where we are Catholic and colourful, you are Protestant and restrained. Where we are crooked and offbeat, you are relentlessly straight and aggressively normal. Where we are hotheaded and filled with swagger, you are falling asleep in a queue somewhere, filled with Pizza Pizza or President's Choice perogies.

There's also the fact that, as a lad coming of age in the nineties and early aughts, I was force-fed a constant diet of state-funded Leafs propaganda on our nation's national broadcaster, the CBC. For over a decade—a lost era that yielded what I term "Generation Sundin"—the CBC banged the drum and led the brainwashing charge in an effort to put forward and lend credibility to the greatest lie in Canadian history: that the Maple Leafs are "Canada's team." How many slightly mediocre Saturdays were Anglo Habs fans like me forced to suffer through where our beloved Habs were robbed of air space in favour of Sundin, Tucker, Lindros and the rest of the old-fart brigade? How many times were we forced to endure the indignity of hearing Don Cherry say literally anything about the Canadiens, on the rare chance that we were actually on *Hockey Night in Canada*? How many nights were we forced to watch weird French yogourt and gas station commercials with strange animation and clown humour? All because the Habs were deemed not Canadian enough to be on the CBC. All in the failed attempt to perpetuate a national myth at the expense of years' worth of alienation for Habs fans.

A divide that had always existed between Montreal and the rest of Canada eroded into a chasm in the nineties. Now, most of this is Montreal and Quebec's fault. Years of masochistic economic policy and taxpayer-funded exclusionist social policy, culminating in the sovereignty referendum of 1995, had forced walls around the province of Quebec, and Montreal suffered greatly as a result. So yes, most of our alienation was self-imposed, or at least our fault. But some of it was definitely thanks to the CBC, who, when faced with a finite number of *HNIC* episodes and a finite number of Canadian teams to cover, followed what they believed to be the smart money and gave air space to the Leafs. Over time, the Leafs, Tim Hortons commercials, Victorian-era period pieces about PEI, *Air Farce*, all of it began to seem more and more like different tentacles of the same white-bread zeitgeist kraken, and less and less like anything close to our experiences or way of life. It all seemed bland and cold, and constantly on the verge of turning moribund. It reeked of wealth and polish and a desperate need for validation from everyone but us.

Every chance flip-over from RDS to the CBC would only confirm this sentiment, as we'd see little pregame short films about Darryl Sittler, or hear Don Cherry wax poetic about some fourth liner from a small town in Ontario I'd never heard of, or hear Don Cherry wax outdated about visors and Europeans. Perhaps it was revenge for years and years of Habs dominance, for Leafs fans having to suffer through us being hockey's golden child for decades. Perhaps it's because the CBC is in Toronto. It definitely was not because of demographics, as the Habs are consistently voted Canada's team in every poll, informal or otherwise. Whatever the reason, we were prescribed Leafs nonsense for years, and all it did was make us more resentful of a team we already hated.

But right now, the thing I hate most about you is that I wish I hated you more. I wish I hated you like I used to. I wish I hated you like my ancestors hated yours. Because I don't. I can't. Yes, you're on the cusp of a potential Leafsian renaissance, brought about by the drafting of Auston Matthews and the acquisition of John Tavares, but your perennial problems remain. As Montreal has hungered, desperately, for a first-line centre for the better part of two decades, it seems Toronto has had an equal hunger for a number one goalie. And defencemen who play defence. My point is that even this new "exciting Leafs" team will most likely succumb to the same, all but inevitable house of cards fate as every other Leafs team since 1967. And that sucks. For though we chirp each other, and cheer hard when one of us scores on the other, it all seems a bit like play-acting. Long gone are the days when either of our teams could be referred to as anything close to the best. For years and years, we have both floundered in our mediocrity, reducing the vast majority of our tilts to little more than our own Punch and Judy shows or Passion plays. Because most of these games are actually meaningless, outside of the immediate petty satisfaction we get from beating our historic rivals. The games might mean something to the fans, in that respect, as a function of romance and novelty, but they usually mean nothing to the actual season at hand. This is because, for the most part, we have both been shit for as long as I can remember. Sure, there have been times when we were hot, or found a way to pull a season out of our asses, but you were garbage every one of those times. Just as there have been seasons where you found a way to be threatening and actually make a go of it, only to have us shit the bed from opening day on. We have either both been shit simultaneously or one of us has been shit while the other was momentarily decent; we have been irrelevant or victims of an ever-shifting power dynamic. Either way, the games between us have been rendered meaningless.

Back when there were only six teams, every game we played against each other was life or death, each of them having a very direct, tangible effect on the seasons they occurred in. As the league grew, we found ways to still need to beat the fuck out of each other, and the Habs vs. Leafs rivalry was constantly reinforced as a result. But as the league kept growing, every wave of expansion just seemed to thin out the hate between us. So we can put on our jerseys and chant our respective songs and chirp our respective chirps, but we all know that any win is just that: a singular win, albeit against a team we have been bred to hate. Even if that hate is now more theatrical than it is real.

And that sucks.

So, in summary, even though I never completely hated you, I definitely used to hate you more. Our hate helped Canada find its voice. I would love to hate you like that again. I think Canada would love that hate too.

I hope to see you in hell.

JB

From: JB [jay@fakeemailforthepurposesofthisconceit.com]

Sent: Friday, April 7, 2018, 19:17 PM

To: de Quebec, Les Nordiques <nordiques@l'enfer.qc.ca>

Subject: I hate you

Chers Nordiques,

Je vous hais.

I hate you. Even if you're dead as fuck, and have been since just before *Batman Forever* came out, even if I never really knew you as an adversary, I hate you. Unlike with the Bruins, I feel no sense of respect for you or fear of you, and unlike with the Leafs, I feel no familial connection to you, nor was our rivalry ever anything close to good-natured. I say "was" because, as mentioned, you're dead. And though that provides some pettiness-tinged satisfaction—the knowledge that you have been dead a long time, the ultimate loser in our epic battle—you still manage to make my blood boil like no other team.

Because you persist from beyond the grave. You live on in the memories of fans and enemies alike, the tragic end to your saga having turned your status as the living embodiment of separatist ambition into full-on martyrdom. Your fucking weird igloo thing continues to respawn itself on sweaters and caps and graffiti tags, and keeps finding ways to rear its ugly face at the Bell Centre, an act that would have been unthinkable at the Forum outside of Derby Day. Basically, you're haunting us. You've been haunting us the whole time. And there's nothing we can do to make it stop. We can't beat you at hockey and put you in your place, because you don't exist. We can't kill what's already dead. All we can do is hate you.

I hate you because I was raised to hate you. As most of my connection to the Habs, and hockey in general, seems to stem from my dad, it's only natural that a bunch of his various hockey-related antipathies would be passed on to me. None of which were half as virulent and rancorous as his hatred for the "Norgeeks," as he called them. His hate for them was all-consuming and specific to Quebec City. Maybe it's because there were no Norgeeks when he was a kid. Or maybe it's because Dad grew up fighting French kids, and separatists, and the Nordiques were nothing if not directly connected to both groups. Not that the Habs weren't—of course they were—but the Habs blossomed from those origins to become an integral part of the patrimony of all of Canada. Yes, the Habs are of vital impor-tance to the Québécois and Franco-Canadians, and are of equal importance to the sovereignty movement. But they are also far more than that, and mean just as much to plenty of people out-side of those categories. The Habs mean what they mean, and then some. The Nordiques fan base was never that diverse or widespread.

There were never Nordiques fans in Saskatchewan. Of course there weren't, and not just because the Nordiques weren't around long enough to export across the country. No, it's because you Nordiques were always focused and narrow and specific in who you played for. There were never going to be Nordiques fans in Saskatchewan because the Nordiques never *wanted* fans in Sas-katchewan. You didn't want to be Canada's team, you wanted to be Quebec's team and did your damnedest to be just that. And in doing so, you inherited all of separatist Quebec's aspirations and fervour, as well as her enemies. Like my dad.

Of course, Quebec already had a team. But you did everything you could to tear our fans away from us, fighting for your place as champions of les Québécois, the Canadiens fighting for the very same, and then some. So right off the bat, a rivalry was born before either of us had played a single shift against the other, just by virtue of the Habs having fans on both sides of the longest, most contentious debate in provincial history. Many rivalries start purely as sport and competition and then evolve to encompass many issues far beyond the realm of athletics. These rivalries become cultural and political. With the Habs and the Nordiques, it was the other way around. This was never going to just be about hockey. This was always going to be fucked.

Familiarity breeds contempt, and our teams really seemed like flip sides of the same coin, right down to our sweaters. And our logos—your weird igloo hockey player thing like a fucked-up, deconstructed version of our CH that was then reconstructed by Belgian art students. We both claimed status as champions of the Québécois. We both played fast, finesse hockey with a mean-spirited, hard edge to it. We were similar but different. We weren't Batman and the Joker so much as Superman and Bizarro. We were heroes and you were our weird negative image, and you were in our head. You still are.

You moved to the States when I was thirteen, so I never really got to experience the emotional spectrum that comes with watching us play you. I did, however, spend all of my adolescence in post-Nordiques Quebec and can attest to the myriad ways you've lived on as an icon of opposition to much of what I was raised to believe.

As an Anglo lad, growing up in Montreal in the shadow of the '95 referendum, my interactions with my city were simple, and binary, and I was older politically than I should have been. I was very keenly aware of a divide within our population, almost sectarian in nature. There was a very real sense of "us and them." The "us and them" meaning federalists and separatists, respectively. This divide played itself out linguistically, geographically, educationally, commercially; there were two sides, and everyone knew which one they were on. Your logo was adopted by the independence movement and has taken its place alongside the fleur-de-lys and the Papineau flag as a sigil to an ideology that I have been opposed to my entire life.

You found and keep finding ways—political, cultural, and more—to maintain a vital relevance in the place many of us Habs fans call home. You endure in contexts where we are helpless to stop you. You've haunted us for many years, and in many ways. Not the least of which is literally everything good that's happened to the Avalanche. Two Stanley Cups, two Presidents' Trophies, two conference championships in the same five-year period, featuring none other than our very own talisman of everything that's wrong with us institutionally, Patrick Roy. Like, seriously, holy fuck, man! We lose the greatest goalie of all time and he ends up backstopping the new version of you fucking zombies to two fucking Stanley Cups. Haunted. Fucking haunted. And you keep fucking doing it.

As mentioned, you keep finding ways to appear at the Bell Centre, on the heads and bodies of people who appear to have embraced the Habs because you're not a thing anymore. And I think that's thoroughly fucked. As if our hateful decade of warfare never happened; as if we were somehow actually on the same side the whole time because we're both in Quebec. We weren't. You and I both know that. You and I both know that something in each of us made us hate the other like no other team. You and I both know that our thing was different. You and I both know that your true fans followed the team across the continent and became Colorado fans. The real ones didn't merely send their hearts two hours south to the next available French team, a team that just so happened to be your most primal and elemental nemesis.

No, the real ones didn't, but the pretend ones did, and they wallow in their convenience as they troll us with their very presence, living and celebrating the contradiction of cheering when the Habs score while wearing the damnable sigil of an igloo that plays hockey. Our encompassing of the less fervent of your rank and file has led to an insidious chipping away of our identity from within, a haunting so prevalent it borders on demonic possession.

And then there is the boogeyman spectre of your apparently inevitable return.

With every new city council agreement or new stadium endeavour, you threaten your resurrection, and it kills me knowing how many self-proclaimed Habs fans will drop our team like a bad habit and return to your weird arms the minute this happens. And I hate you because, God help me, I think I want you back.

I want you back because Canada needs more teams in the NHL, and even though you play for and symbolize the greatest threat to Canada since the War of 1812, I believe Canada's better with you in it. I want you back because I've lived to witness the unbelievable—empty seats at the Bell Centre—and I believe that hockey is only going to get more boring. I think there's a fire sorely missing that I know playing you could provide. I want you back because I know there was something in us that only you could pull out. Familiarity breeds contempt, and there's nothing quite so electric as a local derby. I want you back because hating your adversary is at the very essence of true conflict, and every game between us was a grudge match.

Ours was a pure hatred, the stuff of drive-by shootings and Shakespeare. It was old school as fuck, and the NHL could use some old school. I want you back because Quebec deserves it. And so, this is the ultimate offence you have committed, the apex of your decades-long spectral harassment: you have made me miss you.

And for that, I fucking hate you.

Please come home.

Votre ennemi jusqu'a jamais,

JB

ON SUBBAN, ROY, GOD BEING DEAD, AND NOTHING BEING REAL

LIKE MOST DISASTERS, it felt like it came out of nowhere. Disasters rarely do come out of nowhere, however—prescient observers often articulate what history and hindsight will eventually make completely obvious—but they feel like they do. They have the illusion of surprise, blindsiding us out of whatever semblance of comfortable normality we have settled ourselves into. We feel shocked and heartbroken. The two sentiments compound with and inform each other; the tragedy of the disaster feels somehow even worse because we were caught unawares. And make no mistake, this is the story of a fucking disaster, whose preamble was no different.

I was fucking around on the internet, cramming a bunch of disposable click-patter bullshit into my cortex, when I gave Twitter the ole refresh, most likely to check in on the status of some stupid food pun I posted. My eyes, squinty and dilated, were instantly drawn to the trending list on the left side of the screen. There was the usual shit: #RuinAn80sSong, #BadMonsterMovies, #DolanTwinsNewVideo, Raptors news, and other things that mean about as much to me as whatever Tim Hortons or Budweiser-promoted hashtag they paid to have trend. But all of it was invisible, even more invisible than it usually is, because at the top of the pile were two initials and a surname, and I knew that their presence there meant we were fucked. In an instant, I was overcome by an all-consuming, primordial sense of dread. The kind that manifests itself in squalls of cold rushing through your blood and hordes of asshole butterflies swarming your stomach. My eyes went wide in shock as my hand flew to my mouth. *No way*, I thought. *No fucking way*. And then I clicked on P.K. Subban's name and my whole world threw up.

They (we?) had done it. They/we had actually fucking done it. Boy, had they/we ever fucking done it. The Montreal Canadiens had traded P.K. Subban. Even now, I still can't help shaking my head in equal parts frustration and disbelief, with each emotion informed by a substantial amount of cynicism. Because, of course, we've been here before. Twenty-plus years ago, the Montreal Canadiens traded another flamboyant, hotheaded, walking op-ed piece generator who also just happened to be a generational, franchise player on whose shoulders were carried the hopes and dreams of an entire city, and with whom said city had fallen head over heels in love. And I don't mean Mario Tremblay.

My mum still talks about that fateful night when Patrick

Roy skate-walked out of our lives forever. Aghast and heart-broken and resigned, well aware of the needless, avoidable futility of it all, and equally aware that this was always going to happen, my father turned to my mum and said, "We'll never win another Stanley Cup again." And with that, Patrick Roy was gone, a sweaty middle finger the final coda to not just his time as a Hab—an era that yielded two Stanley Cups—but to the Habs' time as a team that actually meant something. We haven't been to the final since.

They/we chased away and crucified Roy for all the same reasons they/we were attracted to him in the first place. His ambition, his electricity, his inability to do things the boring way. Qualities all, I posit, that we, as a city, seem to pride our-selves on and hold aloft as examples of what makes us spe-cial. Or, at least, what makes us not Toronto. They/we saw these traits in Patrick and fell for him, and then they/we hated him for it. They/we used them as a pretext for carving a god-damned pentagram into our upper thigh. It was a self-inflicted wound, a hubristic act of athletic and strategic self-mutilation. And then, two decades later, they/we somehow fucking did it again.

I remember watching P.K. get drafted in the second round. It was that rarest of moments, when you can actually feel something special happening. Given the genetic makeup of the NHL, and given Quebec's inconvenient history—and pres-ent, really—with minorities and race in general, just seeing a player who looks like P.K. Subban putting on a Habs jersey was cause for, if not excitement, at least interest. Maybe even a bit of inspiration. Seeing highlight reels of what he did in Belleville, knowing his tantalizing origin story—his Jamaican immigrant parents first coming to Sudbury, their love of the Habs stemming from nights huddled around TVs watching hockey with French-Canadian nickel miners—and then hearing him speak only compounded the interest and inspiration. The most seasoned NHL vets usually still give piss-poor interviews, so it follows that most teenage boys lucky enough to be drafted into a professional sports franchise are usually even worse in front of a camera and microphone. This was not the case with P.K. "I'm here to bring the Stanley Cup back to Montreal," he said, and yeah, I'll admit it: I fucking grinned. Here was a kid from Toronto, born of Jamaican heritage, raised as a Habs fan, drafted later than he thought he deserved, telling the whole country that he was psyched to be drafted not just by an NHL team, but by his favourite, melodramatic, crazy, one-of-a-kind sports team. And he was ready to take on the whole world doing it. He had what I, and a lot of other Habs fans, believed to be the requisite ambition to not just succeed but thrive in this club. As a fan of a team that had floundered in the middle of the standings for an entire generation, I found it refreshing to hear someone in our organization talk bluntly and with passion and gusto. P.K. was unafraid to aim for the heavens, and the team was better for it. The league was better for it too, even if it took them a season or two to realize it.

He was given a disproportionate amount of shit. By commentators, other players on other teams, and fans of every team that isn't the Habs. Subban's play was flashy and entertaining, if not multi-dimensional. Was he completely reliable defensively? No, but holy fuck could he create offence. Either way, the ire that P.K. seemed to generate in the opinions of others did not seem commensurate with his failings. A lot of the hockey world seemed to judge him unfairly, especially when players with similar failings and attitudes and on-ice theatrics were not only not condemned for this behaviour but, in some cases, like that of Alex Ovechkin, were lauded for it and the media attention it garnered. But eventually the criticism faded away, due entirely to P.K. having forced his critics to eat their words. Three consecutive fifty-plus-point seasons and a Norris Trophy for best defenceman in 2013 make a pretty compelling argument.

He started quietly with a bang. I remember him lighting it up for Canada at the World Juniors, and particularly a moment in overtime in the 2009 semis when he pulled off a spin-o-rama at the Russian blue line that would've made, and arguably actually did make, Denis Savard blush in appreciation before solemnly and tearfully slow-clapping at his TV. I remember watching with great interest as P.K. tore it up with the Hamilton Bulldogs, racking up eighteen goals from the blue line in one season, to go with a devastating fifty-three-point tally.

And then came his first game as a Hab, on February 12, 2010, against the Flyers in Philly, during which he recorded an assist. This was not a blip on a radar, not a footnote in the storied history of our team; no, this was chapter one in what would be one of the most exciting, entertaining, gut-wrenchingly and mind-numbingly frustrating sagas in the whole of the Habs canon. P.K. was a fucking phenomenon, his on-ice persona and play every bit as exotic and colourful as his sound bites and fashion sense. We loved him for it, even if it drove us crazy and tested our patience more than occasionally. Every time he turned over the puck or failed to get back to our net in time felt like being handed the bill for his offensive prowess. And I thought it was worth every penny.

Not everyone agreed, and eventually the criticism returned—some of it earned, a lot of it a rebranding of the same out-of-date metrics he was measured by during his rookie year. At first, it seemed like yet another case of "us vs. them," which fit P.K. neatly into the Habs pantheon of venerated yet "othered" heroes, Rocket Richard being the most famous but by no means only example. All of Habs fandom seemed to take these criticisms of P.K. as shots fired from foreign powers, and it only made us like him more. We embraced his exoticism because we're exotic. We embraced his flamboyance because we're flamboyant. We embraced his sense of history because we're fucking suffocated by our own. But over time, the shots seemed to wear down a significant portion of our defences, and then it started to happen. What was always going to happen. We started turning on him. Just like we did with Patrick Roy at the first sign of inconvenience. All the keywords of his DNA, the things that drove him to greatness on a consistent basis, the things that made us fall in love with him, suddenly became the reasons why he was letting down the team. Subban's and Roy's individualism was revered until it was resented. Their passions were encouraged until they were punished. Our fervour stoked the fire of their brilliance, and then we used that fire to burn them down. This is the quintessentially Catholic life cycle of la Sainte-Flanelle. This is Montreal in transaction.

Many a diehard fan of many a sports team has similar passions to ours and takes equal issue with what they see as an institutional commitment to wanton societal masochism on behalf of their club—I'm looking at you, Toronto. The Montreal Canadiens hardly have the market cornered on head office and locker room drama. The Habs do, however, seem prone to far more soap opera theatrics and politicization than any other hockey team that comes to mind. There is an obvious reason for this: the Canadiens are more than just a hockey team. Their worth is measured in metrics far more subtle and nuanced than wins and losses over the course of a season. The Habs, as an organization, are in a constant state of flux, purposed by a multitude of interests, each as important as the last. They are an athletic, cultural, political, and often enough, religious institution. And as such, they are beholden to a multitude more criteria for success than any of their counterparts. No other hockey team means what the Habs mean.

And obviously, a large part of why they mean what they mean is because, in addition to being the favourite team of millions of anglophone and allophone Canadians, as well as countless hundreds of thousands outside Canada, they are of and for the Québécois: *les Canadiens. Les Francos.* It was French

111

Montreal, Catholic Montreal, that gave this club to the world. My West End ancestors would have all been avowed fans of the Montreal Maroons, the pride of English Montreal. In fact, the term *Hab* was a derogatory one, coined by Maroons fans as a way of shitting on Canadiens fans, the vast majority of whom were French-speaking. In time, the Maroons would fold and English Montreal would embrace the Canadiens as their club. The term *Hab* would shed all of its bigoted connotations and evolve into a loving nickname for the team that carried the hearts of an entire city, and then of a nation, and then of fans around the globe.

But first the team came from one particular part of the city. This is their team. It always has been. It always will be. It always should be. As frustrating as I find it to know that, no matter what, a huge percentage of the world's best hockey coaching minds will never even be considered for a position with the Habs just because they are not bilingual, I understand, and furthermore agree, that any person hired to coach the Montreal Canadiens should be able to speak French. Just as I understand and completely agree that the Montreal Canadiens should always keep a roster spot or two open for French-Canadian players. Just as Glasgow Celtic will always have ties to St. Mary's Catholic Church and the local diocese and will always keep an eye out for Irish talent. Just as FC Barcelona represents more than just winning; it embodies the very spirit of Catalan independence and thus requires all of its managers to be proficient in not just Castilian Spanish but Catalan as well. Some teams just mean more than others, representing the collective spirit of a minority. The Montreal Canadiens are one of those teams.

That's part of what makes being a Habs fan so damned intoxicating and addictive. You see import and weight and gravity where others just see two teams trying to win a game. You are witnessing the physical representation of a culture asserting itself while also kneeling in reverence to its sacred past. It is mystical sport as a companion for public Catholicism, and public Catholicism reduced to mystical sport. But that's a subject for another hockey book or doctoral thesis. Regardless, it makes for a much more satisfying experience as a fan, especially in the ides of late December, early January, when there is often precious little to get excited about in the NHL.

We get a divine opera through eighty-two-plus games, but pay a steep price for admission. Teams like the Habs are at an inherent disadvantage, as they are competing against thirty other teams whose sole ambitions are, simply and boringly, to win. On paper, if nothing else. In Montreal, even on paper, winning is but one of a multitude of requirements. And yes, there are plenty of times throughout each season when I wonder how much nicer it would be to be, say, a Sens fan, at least in terms of what your digestive system has to put up with every year. Their team either wins or it loses. That's pretty much it. And that's the binary fan experience that most other hockey fans know and understand. For most of us Habs fans, the experience is much more multi-dimensional. We serve other masters than Victory alone. For better or worse.

The other reason the Montreal Canadiens seem to be a petri dish of Shakespearean trauma and controversy is that they are the *Montreal* Canadiens. They are not just a sports team that transcends the values of sports—perhaps by exaggerating them to an extreme degree—they are a sports team that transcends the values of sports in Montreal specifically. The Harlem of the North, the Paris of North America, the crucible of Canadian identity: "Two old races and religions meet here and live their separate legends, side by side," as Hugh MacLennan put it in his iconic novel *Two Solitudes*. It is at once neither Toronto nor Quebec City, and yet is made up of rebel souls from both communities. It has maintained its distinct way of life because it is the last nesting doll from Canada, through Quebec, with difference and distinction increasing with each concentric layer. Yes, Quebec is distinct within Canada, and Montreal is distinct within Quebec. And the Habs are very much from, and subject to, the laws of this particular, distinct ecosystem. Born of Montreal, the CH are beholden to all the same Latinate impulses and nostalgia-bred angels and devils as any other Montrealer. And then some. Like a giant, one-hundred-plus-year-old Mr. Hyde to la Ville de Montréal's Dr. Jekyll, the Habs are a concentrated rendering of our city's collective internal thoughts, a distillation of everything instinctive and elemental about being a Montrealer, set loose first on others and then, ultimately, on ourselves.

We, as a city, see ourselves in the Canadiens. Their history is our history. Their victories are our victories. The monkey on their back is the monkey on ours. As goes Montreal, so go the Canadiens. The two greatest dynasties in Habs history—the fifties team led by Béliveau and the Rocket, and the Lafleur/Savard/Dryden-era seventies team—each blossomed to harvest during ages of great transition in which Quebec asserted itself on a national and then international stage. The 1950s saw the last vestiges of nineteenth-century seigneurial Quebec die out and become replaced by the fervour and electricity of la Révolution tranquille, sowing seeds of sovereignty and independence that would be reaped two decades later with the October Crisis in 1970, and culminate with the referendum in 1980. It also begs mentioning that our last Stanley Cup championship, ivn 1993, occurred less than two years before the province of Quebec once again took to the polls en masse to vote in another referendum on independence. I'm not suggesting the Habs are better for the existence of the Parti Québécois. But for better or worse, the Habs are an extension, a microcosm, and the very embodiment of us as a city and of Quebeckers as a people, and it's reciprocal too. As our defeats are their defeats, the reverse is also true: their defeats are our defeats. We are born with a sense of ownership of the club and, well, it's kind of fucking hard not to take shit personally.

We, as fans, as stewards of the team's culture, wellspring of its lifeblood, enter into all kinds of agreements with the team we love. Some are on paper, like when we buy a ticket to a game or order cable or buy jerseys and merchandise. Others are tacit, like being loyal, or not letting finite factors like success dictate the tenor of our appreciation, or having faith in a five-year plan. In return, we are given entertainment, memories, and the latest instalment of the experiential epic poem that is being a fan. There is a trust and a quid pro quo between team and fan. There is also a security. We are each other's softer place to fall. Transactions like the trade of Roy and Keane for Thibault, Rucinsky, and Kovalenko or the Subban–Weber swap challenge all of that—the former obviously being far less equitable than the latter, though both are uneven.

Part of what makes the Subban–Weber trade unpleasant is that it casts having Shea Weber on our team in a negative light. On any other day, in almost any other trade, this would be a huge win for us. But the contract the team gave up is simply of far more value than the one the team got in return. Like a bad, potentially relationship-ending fight with a significant other, these trades remind us of the fragility and finite nature of relationships we thought were set in stone. They test our unwavering support and threaten our loyalty. They express the true nature of our relationship with the team: it is not a two-way street; the two sides do not answer to each other equally. The team will do what the team does, and they know that we will be here, regardless.

I distinctly remember that awful sensation of knowing there was nothing I could do about something to which I felt so intimately connected. The big decisions had already been made; everything was a foregone conclusion. I was mad as fuck, but worse, I felt like I'd been had, like I should have seen this coming. Falling directly on the heels of that depressing epiphany was the overwhelming sense of having wasted my time. Of having made the twin mistakes of giving a shit about this team and believing that some players—players with what I perceived to be a special rapport with the city—were untouchable. Or, at least, untradeable. Obviously no player is truly untradeable, but I don't know how many Pens fans go to bed at night worrying if Sidney Crosby is still going to be a Penguin when they wake up. Going to bed knowing that P.K. Subban was a Nashville Predator made me question not just who else could be moved, but the validity of watching any of it at all. What's the point? If P.K. can get traded, well then, so can Carey Price, and if that's true, then why the fuck do I give a shit? Why devote hours and hours of my life to caring about and participating in something that doesn't really seem to care if I do or don't?

Maybe I'm insane. Maybe all of this is an overreaction. Maybe I'm a grown man and nobody asked me to care about any of this. Maybe I can just change the channel. Maybe it's just hockey and there are bigger fish to fry. Maybe this team is just a business, like any other team, and I just happen to enjoy their wallpaper more. Maybe it's about profit, not poetry, and there is no inherent drama or romanticism. Maybe I'm just projecting all of these ephemeral qualities onto what should be nothing more than a pastime. But that's not what the team wants, not this particular team. This team knows it needs us to care. It knows that without our obsession, without our taking ownership, without our hearts, it would go the way of any other Montreal sports team that was ultimately just a sports team. This city doesn't suffer half measures when it comes to getting together, because there's just too much else to do. There are too many restaurants, festivals, bars, clubs, parks, protests, and other shit to occupy ourselves with for us to suffer a franchise that's anything less than a religion.

The Habs do need us, just as the city needs us, to fill their respective cathedrals, both literal and figurative. They will just rarely admit it, and they will always own our hearts and will never ask our opinion. Because love is a battlefield and God is dead and all of this is really only as big a deal as any of us choose to make it and we are suffering from Stockholm Syndrome and yet are free to walk out the door. I could never watch another Habs game again, and it wouldn't change a damn thing and no one would notice. So I stay. Because I love them and they're in my heart and my blood and my soul. Because when it's good, when the Bell Centre is packed and it's the playoffs and it's fucking humid outside and 21,273 sons and daughters of Montreal are united and all singing the same songs, all cheering as one, booing as one, when it's good, it's really fucking good, and I can't leave them. And I know that my love for the team and the love that every other diehard Habs fan feels is as profound a part of the experience as the team's on-ice performance is. Our love is the tether to the past and everything that entails. For better or worse.

Because this is Montreal. And everything is a conflict born of two solitudes, and everything is all twelve Stations of the Cross. And nothing ever comes easy, and nothing is ever just the issue at hand. And familiarity breeds contempt, and mobsters make cheaper bridges, and our obsession with history is equalled only by our addiction to romance, and it's −20 for half the year, and ambition is encouraged until it isn't, and the rest of the world is a threat, and blackface is still a thing, and homogeneity is impossible, and othering is an institution, and the Quiet Revolution can never end, and the roads are fucked, and everyone is on strike, and teachers are soldiers with schools for weapons, and the service industry is political, and vice is important, and so is the moment—every moment—and so is the joy of living, and so is humanism and the expression of the self, and no one is born entitled, and everyone is prettier here, and there's no such thing as a bad meal, and all the good art comes from here, and everybody fucks better, and summer still means something, and you're always at the cool kids' table, and you are aware of the memories you are creating at the very moment you are living them, and Canada itself comes from here, and we gave the world hockey, and we have found a way to remove irony from postmodernism.

Because this is Montreal, and Montreal will break your heart. Or maybe it's just hockey and who gives a shit?

FANS

The following short story is a work of fiction.

ONE

Aldo yawned and smoke came out of his mouth. "Fuck, I'm tired." He hadn't done much of anything that day. Sure, he'd gone to Buffet Vichy with Andy and Costa, and then talked shit about how Greek they were to Sandro when he went by Evangelista to pretend to be interested in buying some new Juve zip-up, but really he'd just spent the bulk of his day getting drunk alone and refreshing Twitter. Aldo loved Twitter. He loved lots of stuff, like cars and letting himself go, but Aldo also loved Twitter. He loved being able to espouse an opinion without suffering the consequences of people around him disagreeing with him. Which had been a recurring problem for Aldo; his ability to say things most people disagree wholeheartedly with was matched only by his refusal to deal with his many issues.

Yes, Aldo hated real conflict, but online conflict was one of the only things that made him truly feel alive anymore.

Earlier, Aldo had called someone a retard for questioning David Desharnais's on-ice production relative to his ice time. He had also, paradoxically enough, called the same individual a nerd. And for reasons he'd forgotten—if he'd ever known them to begin with—Aldo had challenged @ScottCrozier14's tacit faith in capitalism by calling him a communist. He took another drag of his cigarette and hoped for a yawn-free exhale. Success. Aldo smiled. And then coughed. He tasted mucus. "Yeccch . . . I'm so tired."

Aldo had spent the bulk of that day glued to his laptop, waiting in vain for a reply from @ScottCrozier14. It was right there with him, perched on the rim of the sink as Aldo smoked and took his second of two shits of the day. And when Aldo finally flopped down for his nap, his laptop was right there on his bare chest, warming his nipples, a helpless vassal of the particular smorgasbord of tentacle hate-manga windows that Aldo had opened in stage one of what was becoming an increasingly difficult ejaculation process. He had gotten there eventually, though, and as he started to doze off, a multitude of questions danced about his fading consciousness. *Is @ScottCrozier14 actually a communist? Did it hurt @ScottCrozier14's feelings when I called him that? How many Scott Croziers are there actually? Did Scott Crozier go to university? Should I have finished CEGEP? Is Saku Koivu nice? Am I racist?* These questions and more swirled about Aldo's soul as, drunk and filled with lasagna, scrambled eggs, and Chinese food, he inevitably passed out hard.

For a brief forty-minute stanza, Aldo dreamt the strangest dream. One in which he was bathing Saku Koivu in Miami, only it wasn't the real Miami. It was Aldo's dream Miami, where all the people were just giant tanned breasts with huge penises for heads, wearing lanyards from an electronic music festival that was somehow also a production of *Mambo Italiano*. His face red and drenched in bathtub sweat, Saku turned to face Aldo, beaming. "You love general strikes." Aldo grinned. "Care Bears." Saku nodded. "I agree with you." Aldo nodded back. "I am your Sun King." Saku screamed, "Your opinions are valid!" and Aldo laughed, safe in the knowledge that @ScottCrozier14 had killed himself. Valhalla. This was Aldo's Valhalla. Valhaldo.

When he awoke, seventy minutes later, his thighs coated in sweat, the first thought that entered Aldo's head was *I get to smoke*, followed shortly thereafter by *I'm a bit queasy* and *Did @ScottCrozier14 reply??* Aldo grabbed his smokes and laptop and plopped down on his couch to check. Bupkes. Aldo shrugged it off; still plenty of time yet for Mr. Crozier to gather his thoughts and formulate a reply. Plus, the Habs were in Ottawa tonight, and Aldo was sure that would create plenty of opportunities for debate. He grinned, coughed, and ordered two subs from Mike's.

And now, eight hours, two subs, six beers, fourteen cigarettes, a Xanax and a 4–3 loss to the Senators later, Aldo was on his porch, smoking and freezing, and still, somehow, he had @ScottCrozier14 blue balls. Nothing. No reply. No sarcastic Like. Nothing. He didn't even block Aldo. It was as if Aldo didn't exist, or worse, it was like Aldo's tweet was irrelevant. Aldo exhaled, and a surprise glob of phlegm catapulted itself up from his chest. "Jesus." Wiping the last bit of spittle from the corner of his mouth, he stared up at the cold LaSalle night sky and wondered if @ScottCrozier14 even knew Aldo was alive. Aldo grabbed his dick and said "Cleavage" without realizing it. He felt futile, and insignificant, and not half as alive as he had not three hours earlier, when he'd gotten to live vicariously through the Habs. Even if they'd shat the bed, it was still their first regulation loss of the season. Aldo was patient; he had faith. Unlike the invisible armies of statistics pussies, who seemed to be looking for excuses to rip apart men he respected, men he looked up to. Real men. That was how Aldo saw himself, as a real man. And that was the exact opposite of how he viewed stats nerds like @ScottCrozier14. They weren't men. They had never played the game. They could never understand or express all the intangibles that real men understood intuitively. Real men like Nick Kypreos. Real men like Aldo.

Aldo farted and his thighs spasmed. "Woof . . ." He let go of his dick and grabbed his gut "Ho-ly fu-u-uck . . ." He could feel all sorts of action and the promise of bathroom time to come. "Lot . . . lot of moving parts . . ." He had been talking to himself a lot lately, and it was giving him cause for concern. Not the actual act of talking to himself—no, Aldo kind of liked that. He found himself agreeing with himself more often than not, and he also seemed to enjoy the same sense of humour as himself.

No, it was that his friends might discover he was talking to himself that was stressing him out. He didn't need that heat. Aldo shook his head and muttered, "No, sir. No thank you."

He started to adjust his waistband, shifting about, trying to divine just what it was he was feeling back there. He took one last drag of his dart and tried to fling it away, but he was tired and his sweaty arms were half asleep, and he ended up just kind of throwing the butt at himself. "Did I fucking shit myself?"

Aldo stared at the moon; he was alone and resenting God. There was much about his life that was contradictory, and a lot that was harmful too. Moments like these, when he felt lonely, yet safe. Sick, yet alive. Depressed, but happy.

Aldo had lots of thoughts he needed to share, and a nagging need for diverse human interaction. Moments like these, when nothing will happen but anything could—these were the moments Aldo liked best.

It was almost 1 a.m. A mediocre Tuesday had become what was sure to be a mediocre Wednesday. The Habs lost, and Aldo had lots he wanted to tell the people on the radio.

TWO

Sean sighed and felt a burn at the back of his throat. He'd taken a Pepcid fifteen minutes before and was still waiting for it to kick in. He burped a weird, almost gasless non-burp and thought, *Fuck*. Tonight the burn was especially bad. He'd silenced the better angels of his nature about seven hours ago, when he agreed to meet up with Corey at Momesso for supper before work. Sean knew full well that he wasn't supposed to be eating anything remotely acidic, and that definitely included meatball subs with chili peppers and beer. But Sean had been in a real "fuck it" state of mind for the past three weeks, and acid reflux prevention just wasn't a priority.

Sean had only really had two priorities during that time, the first of which was making sure that he got to work on time. He was committed to not fucking that up. He'd tried his best to keep up appearances, and keep his personal life in his personal life, but it was all in vain, as everyone at work seemed to know what was up. Sean was desperate to prove that he was fine, even though it was obvious to himself and everyone else that he probably wasn't. Still, he tried, and it took everything in him. Which was fine, because he could use the distraction. He needed the distraction. In fact, distracting himself was the ideological fulcrum of the other of Sean's two priorities as of late: trying his level best not to think about her.

Which seemed basically impossible, save for brief moments of extreme inebriation or obligatory focus on things like work or heartburn. It had been a shitty, and long, three weeks. He'd been dumped before, and dumped others himself, but this one got to him in a massive way, and he'd spent the bulk of the past three weeks meditating on why.

It was because he'd seen it coming and still got the shit kicked out him anyway. That's what he settled on. There had been problems like a motherfucker; they both knew it. Neither of them had been actually happy in a long time. Comfortable, maybe. But not happy. He'd thought about ending it himself many times, and was far more stung and blindsided than he was expecting when she ultimately bailed. And now here he was, sad and lonely and resentful and cynical. He missed her, and he was mad at her for leaving after he'd suffered all her shit, but really he was just bitter that she'd beaten him to it. He was winded, and was seeing the artifice in everything.

Which made his job legitimately difficult. If he'd been a cubicle dude or sold cellphones or worked in manual labour, he'd have been able to just keep his head down and mush forward from a starting point of having zero emotional connection to his work whatsoever. But Sean didn't work in any of those jobs. No, if anything, his was the very business of getting emotional, of giving a shit about something the majority of the world probably hadn't even heard of. And his current emotional state was making it harder and harder to go on the radio every night to talk about the Habs.

Sean sighed again and convinced himself that his insides burned a bit less than they had a few moments before. He hated doing the post-game show; the breakfast shuffle was infinitely easier on the system. But the former suited his current sleeping patterns, and the generationally lapsed Catholic in him appreciated the toll that the graveyard shift was wreaking on him. Not quite penitence so much as appropriateness; he felt like shit, and felt he deserved to feel like shit, and feeling like shit felt correct and familiar. And really, he had no fucking choice anyway. This was the slot he was assigned.

Still, the work itself was getting harder and harder to do. Because lately hockey felt like horseshit. All sports fandom did. All fandom at all, really. It all felt constructed, and thin, and an ultimately silly distraction. It didn't have the weight and gravity it used to. It felt pointless. This wasn't a new sensation for Sean. He'd first started to feel it towards the tail end of his first year on-air. He'd lived in Montreal all his life, and it follows that he had been a Habs fan for the same amount of time. He was a hockey fan in general, and knew his shit enough to have found a way to be useful enough at the radio station to warrant a series of what he believed to be promotions that culminated in his current job on the post-game show.

And like a kid who got to eat ice cream three times a day, Sean eventually started to question the vitality of his interest in the Habs. Usually he just chalked it up to needing a week where he didn't think about hockey or the radio, so he could then come back to it all with decreasing degrees of refreshment. And always that feeling, that the Habs might not be as important as he thought; that the Habs might be as important as ice cream. He'd felt that feeling before, though he'd never felt it so completely as he did right then.

Hockey isn't life or death, Sean thought. The Habs losing wasn't like his personal life turning into a raging garbage fire. *These fools, these fucking people. They don't get it.* Sean felt like he didn't get them, either, and then proceeded to question whether he ever had. How could anybody care about hockey, and trades that will never happen, and conjecture that will never affect the outcome of a single game? How could anybody care about any of this shit when, somewhere out there, there were people being murdered right now? Sean shook his head . . . *These fucking people* . . . and picked at the cuticles on his left thumb.

It all felt like horseshit, and Sean's job was to pretend that it wasn't and make a big fuss out of nothing. Sean shook his head again, and then buried his face in his hands. He smelled cigarettes and the musty ghosts of onion, garlic, and basil. "Fuck's sake." Sean took little comfort in knowing that, as futile and derelict as he felt in that moment, there was no way that this was the nadir of his existence. It would still get worse. It had to.

Likely not during this particular era. No, he would fool himself into thinking he was feeling good about himself and was ready to date, and was not feeling heartburn, and then something horrible would happen. And then the whole dog-and-pony cycle would just repeat itself, over and over again, until Sean eventually got stomach cancer and was then murdered by skinheads during a home invasion. It wouldn't even be a home invasion gone awry. He'd comply with their every demand, politely watching them rip copper wire out of his walls after they'd given up on stealing his sound system because they'd walked there and couldn't carry it all. He'd even keep his eyes closed the whole time so as to avoid being able to identify them once the police arrived. All this, and they'd still stab him to death.

". . . skinheads." Sean laughed ruefully, and though he meant to follow it up with something like "Figures" or "Sounds about right," he actually said, "What a day." Sean realized his error the very instant it happened, also realized that he had just said the word *skinheads* out loud, and then quickly looked up to see if anyone had noticed. Nobody had. Of course they hadn't. They were all too busy caring about silly things like hockey and the Habs to notice people getting murdered and saying "What a day" to themselves. Sean shook his head. "What a d—." He stopped himself and thought *Shit* before recalibrating and saying "Figures."

Sean was overcome with a strange sensation that was becoming far too familiar to him: the melancholy contradiction of wanting a moment to end while wanting it to continue for as long as possible. This is what it is to be depressed. Because now sucks, but at least you know now. And that's how Sean felt about this particular commercial break. He hated it. He hated not being able to distract himself with work. He hated the Brault & Martineau ad that was currently playing. He hated the servile nature of consumerism. He wanted it all to end. Except, of course, he didn't. Because once it ended, Sean knew he'd have to continue marching through his personal fourteen Stations of the Cross, wringing as much filibuster and dialogue as possible out of a 4–3 loss to the Senators that was as boring to Sean as he was apathetic to it.

The game had sucked; the post-game had been even worse. A large part of Sean's job was patience, and he was running out of it. He was meant to be a good host, to stimulate and direct conversation without condescending to listeners and callers. He used to be able to do all that, but he was now drowning in existential futility, and humouring idiots was becoming all but totally impossible. He was fast approaching his wits' end. At least this specific episode of the show was almost done and Sean could soon go home—which was, of course, the last place he wanted to be. He'd recently started referring to it as his "museum of failure," and it smelled a lot like garbage, and he really fucking hated being there.

Sean sighed, again, and looked over at Vincent, manning the boards. Sean resented Vincent. He wasn't sure why, and knew that it was most likely just down to cabin fever and Sean being an asshole lately, but in this moment Sean resented him. Vincent, of course, had no idea of any of this. He seemed blissfully oblivious, laughing at something on his phone. There was a piece of food or something on his cheek.

"You son of a bitch." Sean was saying it to Vincent as much as he was saying it to himself, but Sean was the only one who heard it. "The world is a vampire."

Vincent heard that one. "What?"

Sean became momentarily nervous, then remembered that he was depressed. "Nothing."

Vincent furrowed his brow. "You didn't just say Smashing Pumpkins lyrics?"

Sean stared at Vincent for a decent amount of time before settling on ". . . N-no . . ." as his reply.

Vincent nodded slowly. "Cool, cool . . . okay, well, we're back in thirty seconds."

Sean nodded and said, "Of course," with an odd solemnity usually reserved for talking about grave injustices.

Vincent nodded and eventually looked back down at his phone.

Sean couldn't wait to get it all over with, and yet most of him just wanted to sit here hating Vincent and the chunk of food on his cheek forever. Sean would have hated God too, if he didn't believe God was dead.

THREE

Sean stared down at his phone. It was 12:54, and in six minutes the show would be done. He knew they'd make him jam one more phone call in. He was of two minds regarding the caller he was currently humouring. "Peter" was boring, and was meditating on things that were really self-evident. Obvious truths like "You can't win games if you give up the puck" or "We need more shots on net." Part of Sean wanted to keep stringing the convo out because, as boring and irrelevant as it was, at least it was already happening. The thought of starting the whole process over again, of having to even just say "Hello" to another disembodied stranger who should be doing literally anything other than trying to talk about hockey on the radio at one o'clock in the morning, was almost more than Sean could bear.

But the other part of Sean had had just about enough of Peter. "And, like, when I was a kid, the coach would always say, 'Play to the whistle,' and then these kids today, these are professional hockey players, and all of them are just always looking at the refs, trying to get them to call penalties, when all they have to do is focus on the game. I don't get it, Sean. I really find it mind-boggling. Just play until the whistle. In hockey, you play until the whistle."

Sean said, "Yup," but shook his head before continuing. "Just like most team sports." Sean then mouthed, *You fucking idiot.* Vincent shot a tight-lipped look at Sean. Sean could tell that Vincent thought he was getting catty. Sean could also tell that Vincent had no idea about the chunk of food on his cheek. Sean pointed at Vincent, then tapped his cheek. Vincent furrowed his brow and eventually rubbed his cheek. The chunk of food fell off. Vincent picked it up from his lap and nodded. He looked at Sean and mouthed, "Thank you," and then, gesturing with the chunk of food, whispered, "Noodle." Sean nodded, and thought about how sick he was of Vincent's face, and how Quebec's infrastructure was in disrepair.

Peter seemed to notice the edge in Sean's voice too. "Oh, yeah . . . he-he, I mean . . . you know what I mean, Sean." Sean nodded to himself and googled "Canadian suicide statistics." "Yup. I know what you mean. Thank you, Peter." Sean sighed a silent sigh as Vincent nodded confirmation that the call was done. Sean looked down at his phone. 12:55. *Fuck*, he thought, *Fuck my soul to death.* "Okay, so, I think we've got time for one more . . ." Sean looked at Vincent and hoped he would shake his head no, letting Sean know that there wasn't enough time for one more call and that Sean could go jump off the Mercier

Bridge. Of course, there was no such relief to be had. Vincent nodded yes, and Sean finished his sentence with ". . . caller," while still thinking, *Fuck my soul to death.*

Sean dug as deep as he could. He was running on fumes, and the world was a vampire. He pinched the bridge of his nose and summoned as much energy as he could possibly muster. It was as Herculean an effort as he'd ever put into anything. *I can do this*, he thought. *I can make it through this one last conversation, and then I can go to the bar, where I can continue to google Canadian suicide statistics.* Sean nodded to himself and then looked up at Vincent for validation of this conclusion, as if Vincent could read Sean's mind. Sean gave Vincent a thumbs-up. "Okay, uh . . ." He glanced at his computer screen. ". . . Aldo, from LaSalle. You're on the post-game show."

FOUR

Aldo felt instant nausea, and an equally instantaneous sense of disassociation from his own apartment. He hadn't expected to get through. He'd been listening to the radio after Habs games since he was a kid, and on more than a few occasions, he'd had enough of a buzz on or cared passionately enough about a point to call in, only to hear the callous refrain of the busy signal every single time. And though he was all fired up, and needed to scratch an itch that @ScottCrozier14 refused to scratch for him, Aldo hadn't thought he'd ever actually be on the radio. And now that he was, he was anxious, bordering on stunned. *Holy fuck*, he thought. This wasn't the controlled rush of an online interaction. Aldo was hearing actual human voices. On the radio. And people were listening to them. Worse, they were now listening to Aldo. On the radio. *Why the fuck did I do this?* he wondered.

For the briefest of moments, Aldo contemplated just hanging up, and he felt a slight relief that ended as soon as his eyes landed on his laptop. Aldo didn't have to sit down and click; he knew there was no reply from @ScottCrozier14. Aldo knew there was no reply from anyone. He knew the boredom and aftertaste of understimulation that were patiently waiting for him to get off the phone. Aldo knew he had to talk to people. On the radio. Now. For some reason, Aldo laughed and then said, "Radio." He knew it was weird, and he could tell by the silence on the other end of the line that Sean thought it was weird too.

And Sean did, shifting quickly from confused to annoyed. He looked at his phone. 12:56. Sean smouldered in his captivity and silently cursed everyone who had ever made him do anything. He shook his head and massaged his temples. "Yes. Radio. This is . . . we're on the radio." Vincent laughed. And for the first time in his life, Aldo truly felt close to hell. This was Aldo's hell. Helldo. Aldo knew they were on the radio. Of course he did. That's the whole reason he'd accidentally said "Radio," because he was thinking about being on the radio. Yes, it was a fuck-up, *But, come on*, thought Aldo. Everyone fucked up. Aldo was human, just like Scott Gomez. Aldo liked Scott Gomez. He had so many fond memories of watching him play hockey. *Scott Gomez is a strong name*, thought Aldo.

"Hello?" asked Sean. *Fuck!* yelled Aldo in his head. He felt the sting of failure creeping in; he'd done it again. But Aldo was nothing if not resilient. Or at least, hard to write off. In an instant, Aldo debriefed himself on possible replies. He'd been raised in the backyards, basements, and banquet halls of Italian Montreal, and as such, was used to being disarming while relentlessly saving face. It's what he knew, and it's how he chose to proceed. Aldo would right the mistakes of saying "Radio" because he was thinking about being on the radio, and then being silent because he was afraid, by the simple act of laughing. Aldo did this a lot, because he believed laughing implied that his fuck-ups were intentional. Aldo laughed and said, "Yeah. Yeah. Hello, Sean."

Aldo was overcome with elation. He was happy with that sentence. Sean wasn't. Sean didn't want to be here. At all. And if he had to be here, he didn't want to waste any more time on greetings. "Okay, Aldo. What's up? What did you think of the . . . uhh . . . loss . . . to the Sens or whatever?" Vincent shot him a glance, and Sean knew exactly why. Even he was kind of taken aback by the apathy detectable in his voice. It was like he'd worked out too much and his muscles were finally just giving out. There was nothing there. Sean was all but completely out of chat.

Aldo could feel it. Sean's was the voice of a man uninterested in what Aldo had to say. Aldo recognized it. He'd heard voices like Sean's all of his life, and he'd made a habit of ignoring them, or avoiding them altogether. But not tonight. Tonight he had pushed through his flight responses and found himself on the radio as a result. Aldo was scared, but exhilarated. He remembered feeling like this back when he used to shoplift. He was nervous, and scared, and overly self-aware, but there was no place else he wanted to be. Because Aldo had something to say, and he wanted people to hear it.

"Yeah, so I just want to say that I think there's a lot of people out there who are too hard on David Desharnais."

Sean looked up, surprised by the abrupt ending to Aldo's piece. He looked around, as if there was something he was missing. "That's . . . that's it?"

Aldo was on his feet now. He shrugged. He knew what it was to be alive and smelling every rose. It was as if he'd gained energy from the very words coming out of his mouth. "I mean, like, he seems like a nice guy, and people gotta, like, give him a chance."

Sean's tired discomfort was fast hardening into hatred. He was hanging on by a thread. "Many would argue that David Desharnais gets a lot of chances. Lots of people would say too many. What are you . . . who are you talking about, Aldo? Who needs to give him a chance?"

Aldo shrugged again and noticed that he was getting another hard-on. He nodded, impressed. "You know. Stats people. Nerds."

Something about the way Aldo said "Stats people" really did something to Sean. It angered him. To the point that he looked down and noticed he was actually clenching a fist. "No, I don't know, Aldo. Who are stats people? I read stats. Vincent reads stats. Are we stats people, Aldo?" Aldo laughed, and Sean said, "Don't laugh. Answer the question."

For a few seconds, Aldo blanched, sincerely put off by Sean's tone, which caught even Sean off guard. Vincent was now full-on staring at Sean, worried. And for a few seconds, Sean started to feel bad. He knew he was too angry for his own good. He knew he was almost overboard, but not completely. He knew he could reel himself back in. And that's exactly what he would have done had Aldo not said, "No, no. I just mean, like, I like Scott Gomez too."

This was a night where all professional sport seemed silly and irrelevant, a night where Sean questioned the necessity of his existence, and few things make hockey seem sillier and more irrelevant than talking about Scott Gomez's tenure on the Habs. Aldo could literally have said anything else and Sean might have found a way to keep himself in check. But Aldo said "Scott Gomez," and Sean was losing it. "*What??!*"

Aldo sincerely believed Sean just hadn't heard him. "I said, I like Scott Gom—"

Sean interrupted. "I heard what you said."

Satisfied, Aldo continued. "Oh, okay. Good. So, yeah. Scott Gomez. He's a good guy. Scott Gomez seems like a good guy. Me, I'd make as much money as I could too. I wish I could make the money Scott Gomez makes. Good for Scott Gomez."

Sean was fuming, rocketing towards a full-on mental breakdown. There were few players who embodied the impotent grandeur of the modern-era Habs better than Scott Gomez. His albatross of a contract, and his utter refusal to play anything close to exciting hockey, had been the stuff of many of Sean's opening or closing rants. And Scott Gomez was the last person in the world Sean felt like thinking about. This was torture. Every time Aldo said "Scott Gomez" was like another lash against the mangled flesh of a back that has already been whipped to shit.

Aldo continued, "Scott Gomez is a strong name. Scott Gomez is a good hockey player."

Sean snapped. Everything that was wrong with Montreal, and the Habs, and his life, all the melancholy and corruption and nostalgia and poetry and heartburn and heartbreak, swirled into a perfect storm of cognitive dissonance–induced passion. The entirety of Sean's emotional spectrum was ignited, and he was no longer completely aware of who he was. He knew and understood the emotions coursing through him, and he let his heart and mind articulate them with a firestorm of words. This was Sean's revenge for a lifetime of finishing eighth in the East. "Scott Gomez?? Scott fucking GOMEZ?!"

Vincent's eyes went as wide as his jaw went slack. He was in a state of shock, and was fumbling to deal with the situation at hand. Vincent dropped his phone, then fell out of his seat trying to pick it up, waving at Sean the whole time. "Sean!" whispered Vincent. "You can't swear on the radio!" Vincent wasn't sure if Sean was actually unaware of this fact, but "better safe than sorry" was Vincent's default core belief. Either way, it was to no avail, for Sean's mind and soul were aflame and arcing into the heavens, and there was no pulling them back to Earth.

"You know what?! YES!" Sean yelled. "He's a great player! He's the best Hab in the best NHL because he's the best at being the best!! You know, at least he's honest. You know what I mean? No. You don't. Because, Aldo, you're an idiot. I don't mind saying it. You're an idiot. Please know that I take literally zero pleasure in telling you how dumb you are. Believe me, I'd much rather be comfortable, and satisfied, and off somewhere normal where it doesn't look like the fucking siege of Stalingrad for six months of the year. No, I don't want any of this, but here I am. Here we both find ourselves. I'm telling you what I'm about to tell you for your own good. You need to hear it. All of you need to hear it. For your own good. For all of our own good. We're all dying up here. We're locked in a fucking tomb, and the air is running out, and most of us don't even realize it. Worse are the ones that do recognize it but just ignore it because what the fuck else can we do? You want to know why?

"It's because it's all horseshit. All of it. The NHL, the Habs, this radio station, it's all fucked. None of it actually means anything. None of this is actually life or death. It's all just some silly fucking pantomime that we all put ourselves through time and time again because the reality of our lives is too depressing without it. We are all alone. All of us. And the CH is just the mask our faceless need to be loved puts on.

So fine, let it distract you. Let it allow you to feel like you're part of something, but make no mistake: it's all nothing. *Nothing.* There is nothing actually there. Hockey is not important. The Habs are not important. You are of some importance to the Habs by virtue of you being a customer for them to siphon income from, but there's no actual relationship there. We are entertained, and they are paid; that's it. Same as the relationship between any creep and stripper. Don't believe me? You could stop watching the Habs for the next two years, Aldo, and it wouldn't mean a goddamned thing to them. It's all horseshit. Even this call. I'm being paid to do it, and you waited on hold for free. The Habs are as important as we let them be, and I'm tired of them being important to me."

For a few crystalline moments, all was silent. A heavy silence that felt like it blanketed all of Anglo Montreal. Vincent was still on the floor, frozen in place, like a statue of Vincent. Scared shitless. Sean, too, was kind of scared. It was like he was coming to, snapping out of some weird trance or nightmare. He was hazy and tired, and not entirely sure what he had just said. He knew that, whatever it was, it probably wasn't pleasant.

Aldo just stood there, nodding. He was surprised by just how little taken aback he was. Sean's words had almost no effect on him whatsoever. What little effect there was existed only insomuch as it was a means of inspiring what would go on to be an epiphany for Aldo. And Sean too.

Aldo nodded. "Yeah, you know, Sean . . . I think you're probably just tired. And sad. I get it, bro, it's all good, but you're wrong. The Habs aren't meaningless. It's not nothing. And we're not alone. You're not alone. None of us are. And I think your fucking metric is a bit fucked, because everything, *everything*, is as important as we let it be. That's life. Just like your relationship. I get it, you have heartburn. Your chick left you."

Sean felt a weird rush of adrenaline streak through his stomach. He looked at Vincent and then his headphones. "Did he just say—"

Aldo interrupted before Sean had the chance to finish his thought. "Yeah, that's right. I know about the heartburn. And your ex-girlfriend. It's because I'm a psychic, bro. Seriously, fuck. I'm a psychic, like Louis Del Grande. I know you hate Vincent right now, and you almost threw up in your mouth when he found the old noodle on his face."

Vincent looked at Sean, as weirded out by Aldo's apparent psychic ability as he was stung by Sean's harsh sensibilities. Sean put his hands up, shaking his head.

"Don't worry, bro. I knew there was a reason I called you and got through. I mean, like, I really was just calling to defend Desharnais, but, like, I see that I was meant to get yelled at by you, because now we can both have this epiphany together. So you were right. I shouldn't have called Scott Crozier a communist."

Sean thought, *Who the fuck is Scott Crozier?* before exchanging bemused shrugs with Vincent, who was clearly thinking the same thing.

"Because, yeah, I'm an idiot. That's what an idiot says. And you know what? I think I'm probably racist. I'm examining my beliefs, and frankly, I think I could do a better job of being open-minded. Do you do that? Do you test your beliefs? Do you *know* that you're not racist? I mean, I'll admit, you put a bit of an edge on my name, you know, and you kept saying it, like you were emphasizing how ethnic it was. My point is, there's work to do, always. And I've been avoiding my shit for too long. I live like a fucking hoarder.

"Anyway, I'm just on a high right now because clearly you and I were meant to go through this together. You and I need each other, just like the Habs need us and we need the Habs. We're all part of an ecosystem, and there's no them if there's no us. So look, the point is that existentialism is really just the fucking glass-half-empty or half-full thing, and everything is what you make it, and there's a cynical version of everything, and the world is a piece of shit, but the Habs do bind us, bro. We don't just share the victories. Anyone can do that, bro. We share the defeats. And Orange Julep. We march to the beat of a different drum and take on the world. You know what it means to be a Montrealer in Montreal when the Habs are in the playoffs and our little island is less an island than a whole different planet. If the Habs are horseshit, then so is everything else. But I know you don't believe that. Oh, and don't worry. Skinheads don't kill you. That's not how you die. Anyway, Go Habs Go, and shout-out to my friend Natalie at Cinéma Guzzo."

And with that, Aldo hung up and didn't need a cigarette. Or to go to the washroom. He wasn't tired, either. No, all Aldo wanted to do was tidy. And that's what he started doing.

Sean and Vincent stared at each other for a long time, neither of them sure what to say. Vincent eventually said, "Radio." And then they both remembered that they were still live on-air. Sean was still speechless. He was straining, but try as he might, no words could manifest themselves. Thinking fast, Vincent leapt over to Sean's mike and did what he thought was a good impression of Sean. "Okay. That was so talking. Good . . . night." Sean and Vincent both pretended he'd done a good job, ignoring the fact that he'd said "so talking" because they both just wanted desperately to get off the air. And when they did, they just continued in silence, until Sean finally said, "What a day . . ."

This time, he meant to say it.

FIVE

Sean didn't go to the bar after work. He went straight home. He wasn't sure why, but he knew he needed to. He suspected it had something to do with what Aldo had said.

Aldo cleaned and cleaned until he could see the cold blue of the winter sun start to grow on the horizon. He realized that he hadn't smoked since before he called in to the radio. He toyed with the idea of going outside for one last dart before bed, but decided to just go to sleep, a new day ahead of him, the first day of the rest of his life.

This was the same day that lay ahead of Sean as he finally got into bed. For the first time in weeks, he wasn't at odds with everything, or if he was, it all felt a little bit more manageable. He felt sublimated, and humbled by pragmatism and psychic power. He felt reminded of shit he had always believed to be true, like when his cousin would talk him down off an emotional ledge. For the first time in a long time, Sean was excited about the day to come. So was Aldo.

And as the sun came up over Montreal that morning, Sean and Aldo each drifted off to sleep, knowing that life is what you make it, and that so long as there is such a thing as the Habs, neither of them will be ever truly be alone.

ON FIGHTING

I WAS BORN on Good Friday, April 9, 1982. A little over two years later, on April 20, 1984, the Montreal Canadiens and the Quebec Nordiques faced off for game 6 of their second-round Stanley Cup series, and in so doing took part in one of the most controversial hockey games in NHL history. After a contentious thirty-eight minutes of play that featured a Nordiques goal and a fight between the Nordiques' Wilf Paiement and the Habs' Mike McPhee, and that saw both teams head to the box a combined total of fourteen times, Nordique Anton Stastny and Canadien Craig Ludwig dropped the gloves, and everything went to shit shortly thereafter. As the horn sounded the end of the second period in Montreal that night, both benches were empty and every player was on the ice, beating the shit out of each other. Referee Bruce Hood and his linesmen eventually managed to corral both teams back to their respective locker rooms for intermission without ever officially ending the second period. And after this brief respite, as soon as both teams returned to the ice in the lead-up to the third period, it all happened again.

By the end of the night, Anton's brother Peter would get his nose broken by Mario Tremblay; Habs defender Jean Hamel would be left bloodied and unconscious, and ultimately have his career ended at the hands of Louis Sleigher; brother would be turned against brother as Quebec's Dale Hunter had the unenviable task of having to go toe to toe against his brother Mark; Chris Nilan would seem to fight every single player in a blue sweater; and the officials would dole out eleven different game misconduct penalties amidst a total of 252 penalty minutes taken by both teams. It was Good Friday, and history would forever remember this night as the Good Friday Massacre. Chris Nilan was my dad's favourite player.

This is the world in which I was brought up.

I was never going to be a hockey player, nor was I ever going to be the son my dad envisioned when he found out he was going to have one. That wasn't in the cards, because I never wanted any of that. I hated skating as much as I hated getting made fun of by my peers, and so almost all of Dad's efforts to make me into a better-adjusted version of him were in vain. Some of it rubbed off, though. He taught me how to fight and gave me a relentless streak that has seen me in good stead through hard times.

Dad also made me love movies. His love for that art form was contagious, and I loved the movies he loved, and we fell in love with new movies together. Never was this truer than when I was a child in Oshawa. We were at our poorest, and renting movies was cheap, and every Friday and Saturday night Dad would go to the video store and rent two movies. He and Mum would usually watch them at night, while I was sleeping, and then the next morning I would watch them while they were sleeping. That is, if Mum and Dad didn't deem the flicks too racy for my tender age, which they would let me know by putting a tape back in its plastic case instead of just leaving it in the VCR for me. This system worked, and I almost never broke the rules, because I didn't need to. My folks let me watch way more shit than they didn't, and the result was that I got to watch a minimum of four movies a week from the age of five onwards, a habit which I keep up to this day.

The point is, movies have always been a part of my life and my surroundings, and the only thing on our TV as often as movies was hockey. This was the crucible in which my sensibilities were forged, and though I was never going to be a hockey player, I've been lucky enough to be a part of making two movies about hockey. I met Dad halfway.

I remember getting the call. I was in the back seat of my roommate's dad's Nissan Sentra when Evan Goldberg called me and asked if I wanted to write a hockey movie with him. This is not the canonical, shit-disturbing Evan from my house, but another Evan (Goldberg) that I've known since I was eighteen because he grew up with my buddy Seth. Rogen Together, they've written, produced, or directed a shitload of movies that a lot of people

149

love, like *Superbad*, *Pineapple Express*, and *This Is the End*, which I think is the best of the three movies I just listed, because I'm in it. I'm saying we've all known each other for a while, and I wore Evan's snowsuit and used his snowboard the first and last time I ever went snowboarding.

Incidentally, I fucked the both of us up on said snowboard. It was his turn to babysit me, the rookie, and Seth and their buddy Elisha were off on another slope doing 180s or whatever. Poor Evan was waiting at the bottom of the hill for me. We were all very high, the important difference being that they, as Vancouver boys, had grown up snowboarding all their lives, while I had grown up avoiding situations like this all my life. It was a very poor decision on my part to smoke two joints in a row before locking my boots into the snowboard for literally the second time, the first being in Evan's parents' basement the day before.

Anyway, I got really fucking high and then snowboarded for the first time. As I mentioned, very poor decision-making on my part. I remember being overcome by the combined forces of gravity and velocity as vividly as I remember feeling helpless, and then I saw Evan, standing at the foot of the hill, chatting with someone as he waited for me, unaware that I was heading straight for him. Alarm bells went off in my head, and my heart started racing, as I had to let Evan know that I was about to crash directly into him. But as mentioned, I was very stoned, and in one of the great pot-induced linguistic bed-shitting episodes of all time, the only words I managed to get out were ". . . Evan . . . No-o-o-o . . ." which I'm sure was of very little use to him, though he looked up and tried desperately to get out the way, only to have me barrel straight through him. Anyway, I fucked him up, but fucked myself up way worse, and Cypress Mountain is stained with my shin blood to this day.

Where was I? Oh yeah, right. Evan called me one day and asked me to write a hockey movie with him. He and Seth had had a great deal of success in the States, and Evan had been looking for a movie to make back home. He had been approached by producers Jesse Shapira and David Gross, who had acquired the rights to a book called *Goon: The True Story of an Unlikely Journey into Minor Hockey* by Adam Frattasio and Doug Smith, with the intention of bringing it to the big screen. Evan knew that I was a massive Habs and Team Canada fan, and he knew that I'd wanted to make movies since I was nine. Evan was also one of the only people to read my first script, a 225-page horror behemoth called *The Cult*, in its entirety. The rough rule of thumb for duration and running time in screenwriting is that one page equals a minute of screen time, so at 225 pages, my script was a monster that needed loads of work, and few people had the patience to read all of it. Evan was one of them, and was helpful and encouraging and really seemed to get what I was trying to do, to the point that, months later, he asked me to write *Goon* with him. I, of course, said yes that very second, and that very second, my life changed profoundly, and for the better.

I'm writing this in my "office," which is really just my basement/man cave/prison cell/tree house, and I am surrounded by hockey cards and sweaters—some framed, others hung—pennants, a prosthetic broken lower palate, and a functioning replica of Seann William Scott's right arm, which features knuckles that protrude through skin upon impact in an effort to recreate the look of knuckles breaking, all of it from *Goon* and *Goon: Last of the Enforcers*, the first of which I co-wrote and the second of which I co-wrote and directed. These films represent almost everything that is important to me and has been throughout my life. They are the concrete embodiment of what I've wanted to do since I was a child. They are my service to my country. They are a tribute to my family. They are what I will leave behind, and my life has changed, irrevocably, for the better because of them. And all of it started with that phone call.

Which quickly led to another phone call in which Evan and I came up with pretty much most of what would end up being the movie *Goon*. The ideas came fast and easy, and it was an uncommonly fluid process. We knew what we wanted to say and how we could use this flick to say it. We knew there was stuff we wanted to do differently than in the book, because the book was almost too Hollywood in how it unfolded, even though it was a true story. We wanted to provide something of a philosophical antidote to decades of American sports cinema built around the death cults of victory and Ayn Randian self-worship. Our goal was to tell a story about a guy who finds his calling, and that calling is self-sacrifice. This was meant to be a love letter to everyone who tries their hardest, regardless of any obvious reward; a meditation on effort and teamwork where the entire emphasis was not on winning but on showing up. Very quickly we knew that our way in to Doug was through making him Jewish. I suspect that this was down to two things: Evan having played rugby and competed in martial arts his whole life, always at least a little bitter that Jews were usually depicted as weak in Western culture, and my dad being my introduction to hockey.

As mentioned before, my father lived to fight, and this was confirmed time and time again during public outings throughout my childhood and through myriad anecdotes since his death. I remember being a guest at a Passover Seder when I was like twenty-two or twenty-three. Dad had been in the ground for a few years at that point, and a middle-aged lady at the table looked at me and said, "Baruchel? You're not related to Serge, are you?" To which I replied, "Yes, he was my dad." Now, I feel I should mention that I've had different versions of this same conversation throughout my adult life. Anglo Montreal is small and insular, and we're all of us separated by only two degrees at best. Jewish Anglo Montreal even more so, and when your dad has a rep, it tends to follow your whole family. To be honest, it didn't even start with my dad but with his dad, Johnny, who was as crooked as the day is long and made a career out of dodgy real estate deals and fleeing Canada with other people's money, to the point where, during my father's first court appearance, the judge looked at him and said, "Baruchel? You're not Johnny's kid, are you?" We've been known for generations, and Baruchel was a loaded name long before I ever did anything on TV. Anyway, at the Seder, the lady said, "Your father was my boyfriend in high school," to which her husband added, "I played hockey on the Beth-El Wings with your dad." Now, as someone who had spent his entire life knowing that I could never enjoy playing sports as much as my father, I needed to know just how fucking good he was. To listen to my dad talk, you'd have thought he was one or two bad decisions away from making the NHL, and I needed unfiltered testimony to back that up. The guy looked at me and said, "Your father liked to finish his checks." Which, of course, dovetailed with everything I knew and understood about my dad. He had the fight in him, and he respected others who did too. We revered enforcers in our house, and as passionate and in awe of Patrick Roy as my dad was, no one got him more psyched up than Chris Nilan. I grew up in a house where tough guys were held aloft as a Platonic hockey ideal. It wasn't just Dad, either. Mum loved the fights more than he did, and I have never known a time when hockey fighting wasn't a big deal.

So when it was time to write a movie about hockey fighting, I had a lifetime of fond memories and hard truths to draw from. Not the least of which was my dad's Jewishness, his otherness, and how this dictated the tenor of not just his life but his hockey. And as hockey and hockey fighting are irrevocably intertwined with Jewish culture and the immigrant experience in my head and heart, it follows that our movie reflected that. It was inevitable. Our Doug was always going to be Jewish.

Winnipeg is hard as shit. If Montreal is a snobby, polyamorous Europhile, and Toronto a fastidious Presbyterian dork,

Winnipeg is a stone-faced Prairie day labourer with a chip on his shoulder and a propensity for getting arrested. Winnipeg is consistently ranked as one of Canada's most violent cities, if not the murder capital of the entire country, which it usually is, and was when we were shooting there. It's the kind of place where you could go to an art gallery and a fist fight would break out. This not the sole defining aspect of the city's spirit, but it would be silly not to acknowledge that there is a hardness that permeates the whole place. And a horizon-swallowing gloom that comes from its position at the exact geographic centre of North America. It's windy and flat, and there's usually somebody yelling or fighting somewhere near you. And it's cold as fuck. Like, actually colder than Mars cold, which is a real thing that has happened more than once, as Winnipeg's temperature routinely drops to well below −30 Celsius every winter.

Winnipeg is hard, and Winnipeggers don't have the same opportunities that people do in Toronto, Vancouver, or Montreal. And so they survive, and endure, and thrive. And as happens in other tough places with habitual hard times, Winnipeg creates and finds its own voice. It has as vivid and vital an arts and music scene as anywhere on the continent and has given the world a disproportionate number of artists, from Neil Young to the Guess Who to Propagandhi. Winnipeg, and Manitoba at large, is also very overrepresented in the world of hockey, having provided the lifeblood and rank and file of the NHL and every other league for generations. Like Manchester or Detroit, Winnipeg is a hard town that touches the whole world. Its voice is in its art and in its sport. This is Winnipeg's revenge for being left behind.

And its soul is all over our movie. Because even if the movie takes place in Halifax, Nova Scotia, it was made in Winnipeg, Manitoba, on the backs of its people. Halifax and Winnipeg are not dissimilar: they're both violent towns that are constantly ranked among the most dangerous in the country; they've both lived with economic depression for longer than they haven't; and they're both overrepresented in the world relative to their small populations. Though I set the movie in Halifax because of its role in the romantic lullaby origin myth of my upbringing, simple economics dictated that it made more sense for us to shoot in Manitoba. Film financing is boring shit, so I won't belabour its intricacies. Suffice it to say that it's more affordable to shoot some places than other places, and that's usually what dictates where something will be made. And that's what happened with *Goon*.

But the province of Manitoba's contributions to our film cannot be overstated. We wanted to push boundaries with the calibre of our hockey, and were able to do that because Manitoba is fucking filled with professional-quality hockey players who, for whatever reason, work at the bar or at the shop or fight fires. Billy Keane (brother of former Hab and three-time Stanley Cup champion Mike Keane) and his hockey school allowed a shorthand, an infrastructure, and a standard of play that enabled us to do everything we felt the flick needed. Our director, Michael Dowse, wanted it to be fast and aggressive, and as real as we could possibly make it. Billy Keane and his boys allowed us to do that. They also gave us of one of our actors, Larry Woo, who played Park Kim. I wrote that character as slight and quick and on the finnessier end of the spectrum because I was racist and wrote a stereotype. Larry was at one of our tryouts, helping Billy Keane run the thing. He was the hardest, best player on the ice the whole time, and it was clear that he should be in our movie and that, as mentioned, I was racist. I was very happy to have been forced into smartening up by the sheer, intimidating scope of Larry's presence, because having him on the ice at all times ensured a chain of command and guaranteed that, no matter what, there was always at least one player who could do literally anything we needed done. Most importantly, I can't imagine anyone else playing that role.

Winnipeg provided the vast majority of our crew. Filmmaking was a relatively new industry in Manitoba at that point, and our crew was made up of hard-working, inventive folks who were well up for any challenge before them. We had a shitty schedule, as we were forced into making a hockey movie in Manitoba during hockey season, and the only time that any rinks were available for us to shoot on was in the magnetic arse end of the night. And so literally all of our hockey was filmed sometime between the hours of 11 p.m. and 11 a.m. And it was November and December, and cold as shit, and all of it eventually takes something of a toll. Or at least, it's meant to. But not in Winnipeg; not on our crew. As we traipsed across the province, shooting not just in the city but out in Brandon, Selkirk, and Portage la Prairie, like some kind of fucked-up white-trash travelling circus, these fuck-ing people never complained about anything or backed down from anything. They could all drink like fish, and there were a shitload of drugs consumed from all across the illicit panoply, mostly off-set, but our crew had a seemingly endless reserve of energy and determination, and I'm still stunned at what Dowse and they pulled off. Also, I don't know that Dowse would have been able to slip one of our fighters $200 to take real punches to the face from Seann's double had we shot this somewhere else.

I remember standing by the home bench at the PCU Cen-tre in Portage—which doubled as both the Highlanders' and the Shamrocks' home barn—watching the first take of the donnybrook that follows Doug taking a puck to the face and closes out act two. All of our leads and all of our doubles and all of our utility skaters were on the ice, about to dance. They'd been given instructions, some more involved than oth-ers, and a giddy tension was palpable throughout the rink. These are the moments I live for, when everyone is aware of how cool something could turn out, just like they're aware that its success hinges on them doing what they're supposed to. It was like this on *Tropic Thunder* in the final moments lead-ing up to shooting our first take of the massive battle scene that opens the flick. And it was like this in Portage, everybody amped up and eager to rock and roll, all of our performers lined up with their partners, ready to mime shit they'd been doing or seen other people do all their lives, ready to sell the fuck out of this scene. And then Dowse called "Action" and everyone went to fucking town, and it was all kinds of awesome. I felt the combined thrills of vicarious adrenaline and the awe of something I had imagined coming to life. And my jaw hung agape the whole time.

Sometimes, if you're lucky, there comes a point during the production of a movie when you feel that this moment could be something special. This is not to say that the moments leading up to it have been shit, but that this particular moment takes you somewhat by surprise because everyone fired on all cylinders and the stars aligned and you felt like you were watching history happen. Some moments are more noticeable, if not more important, than others. It's as simple as that. And that donnybrook was one of those moments. There were no actors on the ice, only the characters we were all creating. It was commitment, and truth, and spectacle, and moments like that are the reason anyone ever makes anything.

Or moments like the ones we found while shooting the diner conversation between Doug and Ross Rhea. This was one of the few scenes that stayed pretty much untouched throughout years of development and drafts, and it had always been a personal favourite of mine. I based it on the diner scene between De Niro and Pacino in *Heat* because that's one of my favourite movies and everything I write is *Heat* in one way or another. That's not to say that liking a movie is reason enough to imitate it, so much as it's me acknowledging that part of my scenic vocabulary has been given to me by my favourite flicks, and so, once I knew that Doug and Rhea had to meet each other at some point before they beat the fuck out of each other, I knew that *Heat* would be a wicked way in. It helped me find a way to articulate this purest of our story's philosophical clashes. Rhea's point of view was, essentially, the jaded version of Dougie's: where Doug is all rose-coloured glasses and puppy love, Rhea is all scorn and glass half empty. He was our antagonist, but not our villain. It was a distinction that was important to Evan and me, and one that we committed to very early on. It seemed a more interesting, slightly more complicated place to put the audience in, forcing them to watch two characters that they, hopefully, like almost equally, beat the living fuck out of each other. We wanted the audience to respect Rhea as much as Doug did, and for them to dread having to face him as much as Doug did. We also wanted Doug and Rhea to both be right. Doug's idealism should be as truthful as Rhea's cynicism, and the audience should understand them equally. This was what Evan and I tried to write, and I think we came damn close.

But even if we wrote a perfect scene, that was still less than half the work. Because a screenplay that doesn't become a movie is meaningless. Screenplays are ugly, and utilitarian, and meant to be a manual. The point is, writing the scene gets it to a certain point, but all of its success is still only potential, because the real life of a scene starts on-set. Dowse, Liev Schreiber, and Seann all found something really special that night. For me to try to articulate what that was would be crass, and doing them something of an injustice. What they found is onscreen for everyone to see, and I was lucky enough to watch it happen. I remember standing there, watching the monitors during a take of the wide shot on Liev and Seann at the table, giddy and captivated by all of our ideas that they were each breathing precious life into, and all of the moments of their own that could never have occurred to me. It was snowing heavily, and everyone's jackets smelled like cigarette smoke and winter, and we could be in no other country on Earth.

I remember being in New York, promoting the first *Goon* flick alongside Seann William Scott, Liev Schreiber, and Michael Dowse. Liev said something during one of the interviews that day that struck a profound chord with me, and as is the case with all ideas that land hard and feel personal, I think about it still and have done since he said it. The interviewer had asked some version of the "What's the deal with all the fighting up there?" question. This was something of a recurring theme as we brought the flick south of the border. For a lot of Americans, hockey and hockey fighting seemed novel, somehow both foreign and familiar, and seemed to go against whatever combination of labels they had previously decided best described Canada. Like remembering that your nerdy cousin is part of a backyard fight club. Americans always seem at least a little caught off guard when they see us whaling on each other. They're not impressed so much as weirded out or confused. Because America's culture is steeped in military fetishization to the point of being a death cult, and it achieves whatever international legitimacy it might have in large part by expressions of force, and none of this is true of Canada. Our brand is quiet pragmatism and peacekeeping. As Liev said, "There's something incongruous about Canadians, who are so sweet and polite, and yet capable of such extreme violence." I'm paraphrasing a wee bit, although I distinctly remember him using the word *incongruous*.

The point is, he was right, and he had hit on something that I had always known subconsciously but that had never actually occurred to me. Probably because I'm Canadian and have lived here for most of my life, and things like that need an outsider to see them. It's like having a weird relative, and you know they're weird, but when your friends meet them, you realize they are actually insane. I had always known that we liked watching fights, and getting into one was never a big deal for anyone I knew, just as I had always known that Canada was, on balance, clean and safe and compassionate. It just never occurred to me that these ideals and phenomena might somehow be contradictory. And I had written a whole fucking movie about hockey fighting.

We're obviously not the only country in the world where people dig fighting. Fighting is universal and ancient. As long as there have been people, there have been people beating the shit out of each other while other people watch. This is true everywhere. There is not a country on Earth where fighting doesn't exist, nor is there a country on Earth where it is unilaterally condemned. But different cultures have different relationships with violence. There are neighbourhoods across the world where warfare and death are everyday occurrences and hurting one another is a function of being alive. Other neighbourhoods are funded and protected and free of those problems.

Mercifully, I was born into a country made up of the latter. I didn't grow up amidst ruins, and I have never seen someone get murdered in real life. I am fortunate enough to have been raised in a country that is, by Western standards, safe, and by global standards, a paradise. We are educated, prosperous yet cared for, and protected from most of the ills we see plaguing other countries on TV. People from across the world flee violence and choose Canada precisely because it has so very little of it. Canada has, for reasons like affluence, opportunity, and isolation, been allowed to excise violence from its streets, and our founding principles of "peace, order, and good government" are still a Rosetta stone to Canadianism. For all intents and purposes, we have, as a country and a society, evolved past institutional violence. Why, then, do we enjoy watching it so much?

Maybe it's because most of us love stories, and every fight tells one. Any story is born of conflict, and there is no purer distillation of conflict than a physical confrontation between two relative equals. We can project our emotions onto any fight, imbuing the conflict with motivations and ramifications that are significant to us, and in so doing, we elevate the experience. We have a favourite, and thus there is a hero and a villain. In a hockey fight, there is often no projection required, as the sweaters do all the work for you. You had a favourite long before anyone knew there was going to be a fight. And then the fight breaks out and the stakes are like that of a comic book, only way fucking higher, because you know Batman will usually win, but this is real life and anyone can lose a fist fight. Especially on skates.

When we watch a fight, we are seeing living, bleeding examples of determination, presence, and willpower. We are watching extreme incarnations of experiences we all understand in one way or another. We have all been afraid, we have all been angry, we have all been hurt. And so, when we watch two people experience all of those things simultaneously, and on a scale for which many of us have no equivalent, we know just how incredible and worthy of note moments of inspiration are in that setting. To persevere, and maybe even succeed in spite of bodily harm or the threat thereof, is to inspire a stadium full of people and make heard your voice across the whole of a country.

We watch a fight because we want our guy to succeed. We want our guy to succeed because we want our team to succeed. We project our hopes and our failings onto the shoulders of our fighters, and we live vicariously through them, our fates hinging on their actions. We give them our flag, and knight them our champions, and they will inspire us, or they will disappoint us. We watch fights for history, and for the future, and for entertainment, and for victory. In other words, we watch fights for the same reasons we watch hockey or any other sport. Their importance is purely contextual, and they are as much of a thing as we want them to be. Just like hockey. Just like anything, really.

Why do people hate fighting? Well, let's start with the fact that the sport of ice hockey really has nothing to do with fighting. We know this because hockey games are won by goals scored and seasons are conquered by points earned, and fighting isn't scoring goals, nor is it worth any points whatsoever. In fact, it's penalized and would seem to be a hindrance to a team's success, if anything. Most hockey games in the world are played without anything more than a slight tussle at the whistle, and nowhere outside of Canada and the States is fighting's effect on the outcome of a game debated or even humoured. Because, almost everywhere else in the world, fighting is as relevant to hockey as an apple is to an orange. Because the object of playing hockey is to score more goals than your opponent and not to win more fights than they do.

So people who grow up on this side of the world and enjoy watching hockey but think fighting should be taken out of the game are most likely exasperated and frustrated by the fact that there even has to be a debate about something so self-evident. Like Americans in favour of universal health care, these people must feel something close to embarrassment at just how out of date this side of the world is. They might very well enjoy watching boxing or mixed martial arts, because those fights exist in a context where they themselves *are* the context. Hockey is hockey; hockey is not fighting, so why the fuck is this even a thing? The frustration and exasperation must be compounded by the apparent inability of the proponents of fighting to defend their position with any argument that could actually be called concrete. There is lots of talk of momentum and X factors and codes of honour and fans being on their feet, but nothing quantifiable. There are no metrics for any of it, and no one can defend fighting with anything they can prove. It's all romance and instinct, and it must seem straw man as fuck. To its opponents, fighting's irrelevance is confirmed by its failure to be adequately justified.

It's most likely further corroborated by the inherent ethical risk and hypocrisy of fans enjoying and encouraging violence and pain and then being shocked or solemn when something bad happens to one of the players. Every staged fight, shared highlight, and validated display of brutality must only prove to fighting's opponents how ugly this whole relationship between fans and enforcers is. Each generation gives us a certain class of men who will hurt and get hurt and then be spit out by hockey somewhere slightly north or south of the age of thirty. Even if they were heroes during their time in the big show, and remembered fondly by their fans, time and violence will have taken their toll, while those same fans will have turned their attentions to someone else. Their fans may pay homage and respect to them in one way or another, they may even acknowledge that there is most likely some correlation between fighting and dysfunction, but when faced with the simple question of whether fighting should be allowed in hockey, they will still say yes.

This truth must spur on some degree of moral imperative in the effort to rid hockey of fist fights. Especially if you are someone who doesn't enjoy or appreciate fighting of any kind, in any context. Which would be understandable, as all of Western society's institutions, from school to the church to the government, seem focused on the singular task of ensuring peace and safety, which, of course, means preventing and discouraging violence. From childhood, we are raised to believe that violence is wrong and not to be celebrated, and all of civilization is meant to be built on that principle. Violence is not only discouraged, it is illegal, and so people who abhor it in all forms must be especially put off by its welcome prevalence in hockey and our culture at large. Violence and pettiness and tribalism are meant to be failings to be exorcised from our daily lives. How can we allow and even celebrate something that people go to jail for?

Or do people hate fighting because the entire ecosystem of violence—fighting, fighters, addiction, shame, pride, glory, repercussions, rewards—is a more vivid, distilled version of the entire ecosystem of professional sports? Hockey fans who hate fighting for all the reasons just listed could logically be expected to take issue with hockey itself. Hockey is a contact sport, and bigger pads haven't made the game safer. If anything, players are openly bodychecking the fuck out of each other as much as ever, if not more so. There are myriad ways for a hockey player to sustain a concussion, many of them "clean" and unimpeachable. Guys can get fucked up a whole bunch of legal ways in hockey, with long-term effects that are often similar to those suffered by fighters.

The game of hockey is, by its very nature, a violent one. Any game that allows and encourages physical contact is a violent one. Many hockey players will go their entire careers without getting into a single fight, and their bodies and emotions will still be brutalized, and they will still see themselves spit out by hockey a little north or south of the age of thirty.

And the fans might have loved them, might love them still, but their fans, too, will move on to the next guy.

The point is, all of pro sports is an ethical risk. All of it is, arguably, an uneasy relationship between what one believes and exemptions one makes for one's favourite athletes. Competitiveness may not be a sin, but it is hardly a virtue either, and it, along with greed and pride and vanity and tribalism, is not just on display in pretty much any professional sport in the world, but is a defining aspect of sports. An athlete needs not just the will to win, but the overwhelming desire to. This is what we expect of them, what we require of them. We require them to be greedy on our behalf, because we want them to win as much as they can. We require them to be proud and to honour their sweater, and we hold particularly dear the team members capable of moments of individual brilliance. We require them to sacrifice their lives and their bodies for the glory of our neighbourhoods.

What is also required of most professional athletes is a lifetime of isolation, expectation, and pain. We fall in love with them, then just as quickly turn on them; we use them as proxies and take ownership of their successes only to distance ourselves from them whenever our fandom becomes inconvenient. We reward their dysfunction and their corporeal sacrifice, and then pay our respects whenever some poor bugger gets stretchered off the ice. We all know full well how common addiction is in non-traditional careers like hockey, and we can all have a realistic expectation that people who choose to feel adrenaline for a living might not be homebodies or wallflowers on their days off. Maybe some of the distaste for hockey fighting comes from hockey fans knowing deep down that the whole ecosystem of the sport exists in something of a moral grey area, and cheering on a hockey fight holds a mirror up to all of it. It is a vivid example of how the sausage is made, and its existence threatens the palatable narrative of consequence-free hockey.

I can understand and appreciate why people hate hockey fighting, just as I know how futile it would be for me to protest where history has already decided to place it. It is all but extinct, and though I miss it, I can't argue against any of the reasons people dislike it. Even if I know that, really, they just don't like watching it and never did. Just as I can defend and explain and try my best to provide justification or at least context for hockey fighting, but really, I just like it. I always have. I'm sure this will come as no surprise, as I have co-written two films and directed one centred around hockey fighting. My enjoyment and appreciation of fighting isn't limited to on-ice tilts either. I watch the UFC, K-1, boxing, Worldstar Hip Hop street fighting compilations—all of it. I also love fight scenes in movies, and will routinely call my favourites up on YouTube to show to whomever the fuck will let me. I love punches and kicks and head-butts and body slams. I dig watching all of it, and have done since I was a kid.

There is a very true and sincere tradition of fighting in hockey in our country, going pretty much as far back as the game's birth. Literally the very first time that hockey was ever played indoors, there was a fight. A big-ass one too. On

March 3, 1875, at Victoria Skating Rink in Montreal, the very first organized hockey game took place, and it resulted in a fucking donnybrook. This is not proof of fighting's validity in hockey, nor is it a sophistic little footnote. It is, however, a very real example of the fact that people have been fighting during hockey games for as long as they've been playing them here.

But even so, I understand why people hate it and why its very existence has been challenged into extinction. I can make no arguments for its merits that aren't at least a little tinged with emotion and romance, nor can I say that it has no tangible positive effects on the game whatsoever. But what I can and must acknowledge is the fact that fighting in hockey and all that comes with it—the blood lust, the suffering, the moral and ethical debates, the contextual heroism and villainy—all of this is the stuff of drama and storytelling.

On September 10, 2011, *Goon* premiered at the thirty-sixth annual Toronto International Film Festival. It was obviously a special day for all of us involved. We had worked our asses off on this flick for years, literally, and the reception was commensurate with our efforts. People legitimately seemed to dig the movie. Every joke and every punch landed with all the weight we'd hoped they would, and the screening ended with a five-minute standing ovation. Which was fucking crazy, and beyond our wildest dreams. That standing O also served as a portent for the rest of *Goon*'s life, as roughly six months later, we would open across the country at number one at the box office. This in spite of, or possibly because of, a silly bit of made-up controversy involving posters with my face on it.

Basically, people in Yorkville or whatever didn't like seeing me making the cunnilingus gesture, as I was doing on my character posters for *Goon*, and they got the city of Toronto to pull all of said posters from every bus, bus stop, subway station, and billboard across the city. A day later, Montreal followed suit. We were annoyed for a second, because it was the week our movie was coming out, but we quickly realized that this nonsense and all the weird press it had generated was only helping us sell tickets.

Anyway, we opened at number one at the box office, across Canada, and I don't know the last time that happened. *Bon Cop Bad Cop* is the highest-grossing domestic Canadian film of all time, but the bulk of those tickets were purchased in Quebec. Because the Québécois watch their shit and know that a culture can't rightly be called a culture if it has no voice. Quebec can make movies about Quebec, and Quebec can make movies about Quebec successful. English Canada is an entirely different ballgame. For generations, English Canada has gone to the movies to watch stories about other people. That weekend, English Canada went to the movies to see themselves.

Temerity and self-importance notwithstanding, we set out to make a good movie for Canada, and Canada let us know that we not only did a decent job, but were right in our belief that Canada deserved to be reflected in its cinema, that Canada deserved to be more than just a waiting room for other cultures' ideals. You always hope for the best but never take it for granted. And so we were shocked, but not surprised.

Because we had always believed in the flick and knew it could go toe to toe with anyone. Which it did, and continues to do to this day.

All of it started on that day in September of 2011. We were all asked about a whole bunch of stuff on the red carpet that afternoon, most of it innocuous, like "What are your favourite restaurants in Toronto?" or "Have you seen any movies at the festival this year?" or "Were there any on-set pranks?" Some of the questions were slightly more substantive, centred around the novelty of us having actually made a) a hockey movie and b) a Canadian movie that didn't try to bury its citizenship. These were questions like "Why set a movie in Canada?" or "Why come back to Canada to make movies?" or "What's your favourite hockey movie?" That last one isn't exactly substantive, but I'm writing about memories of events that happened over a half-decade ago, so these are all fairly composite anyway. In other words, these may not have been, verbatim, the questions asked of us, but they were all definitely in that vein and indicative of what was on everyone's minds that day.

There was something else on everyone's minds too, or most people's, anyway. I know I was certainly well aware of it. It was kind of hard not to be. I'd have had to be ignorant, and callous to the point of sociopathy, to be unaware of the fact that former NHL player and career enforcer Wade Belak had died at the age of thirty-five less than two weeks earlier, on August 31. The tragedy of his death was vulcanized by the fact that it happened in the same year as the deaths of two other

NHL tough guys, Derek Boogaard, who had died of an overdose on May 13, and Rick Rypien, who had taken his own life sixteen days earlier than Belak, on August 15. Their deaths had put mental health and the effects of post-concussion syndrome in the spotlight in a way that Canada hadn't experienced before. It would be possible for someone to dismiss any of these deaths as flukes or anomalies had any of them occurred in a year unto themselves, uninformed by the corroborating existence of two other tragedies so eerily similar in their demographic makeup. It would be possible, albeit heartless, to write off any of the deaths individually as some degree of coincidence. But when three men who are roughly the same age, who are from roughly the same ethnic and economic backgrounds, who perform the same job as one another, which just so happens to be one of the most specifically violent jobs on Earth—when these men battle roughly the same demons and each meets roughly the same tragic end, it is very hard, bordering on impossible, to deem any of it coincidental.

Yes, suicide is different from accidental overdose. I know this because my father died of the latter. But I also know that happy people don't die of accidental overdoses, and Derek Boogaard, like Serge Baruchel, had battled depression and the demons in his head for a long time. All of them had. And the deaths of the three players forced Canada, and the world, to acknowledge that something might be wrong—or, at the very least, that something was happening and worth acknowledging. Mental health is still burdened by the stink of stigma, and we, as a society, have yet to normalize it properly. We get closer and closer every year, but the fact remains that most people can't afford a shrink, and if we actually believed mental health was as important and remediable as any physical injury or affliction, therapy would be universally accessible. But it isn't, and being sad or fucked up is still something of a dirty little secret. Especially when it comes to professional athletes.

As mentioned, there should be a reasonable expectation that someone uniquely focused and talented enough to play hockey professionally, a person who has devoted so much of their mental and emotional real estate to one task alone, has less time and space to be normal. For most people, work is one of multiple issues of equal importance. For a professional hockey player, like a professional musician or a professional actor, work is almost the entirety of their existence, and so it follows that they have that much less time and energy and ability to function in normality. This is not to say that every NHLer is a mess like I am; I'm sure a significant portion, if not the majority, are well adjusted and find a way to keep their demons at bay or in check. Nor is this to say that moral exemptions should be made for people just because they do a special job for a living that makes them famous. It is merely to say that if mental health is an issue that affects most people who don't play hockey for a living, it follows that those who do would be even more at risk.

The tragedy of these deaths also brought back a discussion about the merits and validity of fighting in hockey, period. Derek Boogaard, Rick Rypien, and Wade Belak were fighters. *Fight* was the defining verb of each of their hockey careers, and the nouns would have been *enforcer* for those who respected what they did and *goon* for those who didn't. For better or worse, these men fought for a living, and they all met a similarly tragic and abrupt end far too soon. Each had a family that they left behind. Each had lives made up of triumphs and defeats, joys and sorrows, boredom and excitement, and friends and enemies, all of which were left behind to be analyzed and prodded in the public eye. Like anything worth examining, the personal demons of pro athletes weren't new to us, but were issues we, as a society, had known about for a long time.

I met John Kordic when I was four years old. I was walking through the airport with my dad when he spotted Kordic, leaning into a conversation on a pay phone. Dad told me to go up to him and say "Hi, slugger," and I did. Kordic grinned at me and gave me either a thumbs-up or a high-five. Or maybe both. He was one of my dad's favourite players, and watching old highlights of his during my adult life has shown me why. He was a fucking force of nature who routinely felled bigger, more experienced men than himself, and that year, his first in the NHL, he got his name on the Stanley Cup as a member of the 1986/87 Montreal Canadiens. Six years later, John Kordic died, on August 8, 1992, his lungs failing him after he overdosed and fought police at a motel outside of Quebec City. He was twenty-seven years old.

There was another member of that Stanley Cup–winning hockey team whom history has remembered more for his fists than for his ability to skate or score goals, neither of which was actually all that poor. By the time 1986 had rolled around, Chris Nilan had firmly established himself as an intrinsic part of the best team in the world, and his fists had given him the nickname "Knuckles." Dad loved Kordic, just as he loved Roy, Robinson, and Gainey, but his favourite was Chris Nilan. Knuckles was less a fighter than a superhero, and his penalty minutes always read like area codes. Nilan got his name on the Cup with Kordic in 1986 and would go on to play another five seasons, three with the New York Rangers and a season and a half with the Boston Bruins, before coming back to Montreal to end his career as a Hab. Which is not insignificant, considering that he was a lifelong Bruins fan from Southie. Nilan had a monkey on his back for most of his career, but it was after hockey that shit really got difficult, culminating in him becoming addicted to heroin in his forties. He has since conquered his shit, and is now quite proud to speak about his struggles; he seems determined to make them transparent, in an effort to save someone else from having to go through what he did.

I have been fortunate to call Chris Nilan a friend for the better part of the last decade, and on July 25, 2013, he joined me onstage at the Salle Wilfrid-Pelletier at Place des Arts for my gala at the Just for Laughs festival. I had a bunch of bits that my writing partner and I came up with, which were really just a means of keeping the audience entertained between actual funny people doing their thing. As host, my job was just to keep the machine running, and by the time we finally put the show on, we had rehearsed and revised it to the point where I knew it all like the back of my hand. Or so I thought. I was on my way out for a smoke when someone stopped me and told me I would probably want to see what happened next. The room went dark, and onscreen appeared Geoff Molson, president and co-owner of the Canadiens, holding up a Habs sweater with my surname stitched on the back. He was naming me an honorary captain of the Montreal Canadiens, and as if that wasn't enough to get me all choked up, he then introduced Chris Nilan, who walked out onstage with said sweater and presented it to me. At which point I got down on my knees and hailed him before rousing the audience to give Nilan the ovation he deserved. He was Dad's favourite, and here he was, almost a decade after my father died of a drug overdose—Nilan himself a survivor of addiction—presenting me with the symbol of my captaincy of the Habs. The audience roared and gave him a hero's due, all the while knowing what he had done for a living. They applauded him not in spite of it, but because of it. He was a hero, and he still is, and like any hero, Nilan is a human being, and flawed. His personal life suffered at the cost of his professional one, all so he could inspire a generation of Habs fans.

He was flawed, and human, as all of them were. These men were hockey fighters, and they were all suffering inside their own heads, and the logical follow-up question is: Were they suffering *because* they were fighters? I don't know. I am not a scientist, psychologist, brain surgeon, or sociologist. I have no medical or scientific context in which to place any of this. Most importantly, I am not a hockey player, and I can only ever live that particular experience vicariously. I can observe, and try to find equivalency, but at the end of the day, it is all theoretical.

For me to say there is no connection between what these men did for a living and the horrid end that each of them met would be obtuse and an affront to everything they and their families have suffered. It would be equally inappropriate for me to definitively say that these men were broken by their jobs. Because the proximity of their deaths is jarring, but the majority of NHL fighters haven't met the same tragic fate. That doesn't change what happened, or change the fact that what they all went through needs understanding and appreciation; it just means that their experiences are not necessarily representative of all fighters. How could they be? No one person's experiences are representative of everyone's. Still, there are commonalities and patterns, and if we're going to watch these people do what they do for a living, then we are obligated to understand what they are living through. So, ultimately, I don't know. I don't know that these men suffered because they fought, or if they fought because they suffered, or if it was somewhere in the middle. I know that they suffered, and that their suffering was real, just as I know that they were heroes and their ability to inspire was real.

And so, on that afternoon in September, the lives and deaths of Derek Boogaard, Rick Rypien, and Wade Belak were on our minds. Like I said, I'd have to be a huge fucking asshole to not think about them. And the media, rightfully, asked us what we thought, tried to pinpoint where our responsibility might lie in this. After all, we had made a movie about hockey fighting. Were we glorifying something that was profoundly affecting people in a negative way as of late?

It's not a sophism to find a distinction between romance and glory. One can romanticize something, crystallize and heighten it for artistic consumption, without putting the entirety of one's weight behind endorsing it. And that's what I believe the *Goon* films do: they romanticize and make operatic one of the world's weirdest jobs; they show what's admirable and worth lauding about it, while also showing how intrinsically fucked it all is. The films exist in a grey area. Doug is a hero, but I don't think anyone walks out of our movies thinking they were a recruitment ad for a life in violence. We show what's lovely about hockey fighters, while also showing how broken and sad their lives can be. If you dig hockey fights, our flicks articulate just what it is about them you enjoy. If you hate them, then our flicks show you everything ugly and pointless and institutionally cynical about them.

The *Goon* films exist in a grey area because hockey fighting exists in a grey area because hockey exists in a grey area because all spectator sports exist in a grey area. Sports are made up of winners and losers, and all those winners and losers are heroes or villains depending on what city you're in and what day it is. And all of them—the winners, the losers, the heroes, the villains—all of them are human beings. So, while a film can end with a two-dimensional character going off to tend to their two-dimensional wounds in the abstract comforts of imagination, a hockey game will end with real people tending to real wounds in the cold discomfort of reality.

And even though every informal player poll confirms the sensation that anyone who has ever watched a fight in the Bell Centre knows—that fighting is every bit as electric and vital as any other aspect of hockey—it is an all but extinct pastime. Society has put to intellectual bed a debate that was always more about emotions than thoughts anyway. Hockey fighting is dead, and its place is in history. We have, as a civilization, decided that we cannot endorse it. We can lament it, and forge golden its merits and heroes, but it is gone. That lament is justifiable only if we acknowledge what fighters look like once they go home. Some will conduct business as usual; others will struggle. Theirs was a violent job, and they were instruments of therapy for an entire culture. Many of them had their hearts broken by the game they loved so dear, and their violence is sadness. Others lived their wildest dreams and then some. The rare few lived for the sensation of the fight itself. Most were probably somewhere in the middle, doing an ugly job for boys and sweaters they loved. They lived a life outside expectation and status quo.

Is hockey better off without fighting in it? Who knows? I could say getting rid of it has made the game boring, but that would be unfair. I think fighting's end is more of a symptom than a cause, just one of many differences between the game now and how it used to be played. The modern NHL feels more boring, with less at stake. Games drone on while somehow being more cynical and cold than they used to be in terms of physical contact and violence. But these are feelings. They are not facts. So is the NHL better off without fighting? I don't know. Is society better off without fighting in the NHL? I don't know that, either. Time will tell.

What I do know is that it was real, and sincere, and proprietarily Canadian. Hockey fighting is Canada's martial art, and it would be hypocritical of me to deny how much pleasure I have gotten from watching it over the years. Yet I know how much stress it has caused and how ugly it must have seemed to so many other people for so long. Whatever one's opinion of it, one cannot deny that hockey fighting is as sincere a manifestation of Canada's soul as we've ever known, with all the beauty and all the ugliness that entails. For, as ugly a job as being an enforcer was, the beauty that it allowed is nothing if not worthy of emotion and respect.

Because Patrick Roy never got the Habs logo tattooed onto his flesh. Neither did Rocket Richard, nor Guy Lafleur, nor Bob Gainey, nor Saku Koivu, nor Alexei Kovalev. Not even P.K. Subban, whose love for the Habs was unabashed and uncommonly public, could defy reason and logic with passion enough to tattoo the team he played for onto his very body.

But Chris Nilan did.

TIMELINE OF THE GOOD FRIDAY MASSACRE

April 20, 1984.
Game 6 of the first-round playoff series
between les Canadiens de Montreal and les Nordiques de Quebec.
Montreal leads the series 3 games to 2.

FIRST PERIOD

00:00:23

After a scrum against the boards, QUE #27 Wilf Paiement and MTL #35 Mike McPhee scrap behind the Quebec net and receive offsetting majors of five minutes apiece. It is a brief, anticlimactic portent of what's to come.

00:02:48

MTL #15 Bobby Smith and QUE #16 Michel Goulet incur

offsetting minors. Smith for slashing. Goulet for holding. Two minutes apiece.

00:04:28

MTL #17 Craig Ludwig gets two minutes for tripping QUE #26 Peter Stastny. Quebec had not scored a power play goal against Montreal in the last twenty advantages; they were one for twenty-two in the series and had had three power plays where they couldn't manage a single shot on net. Incidentally, Montreal had only been three for twenty on the man advantage against Quebec in the series thus far.

00:05:01

MTL #28 Jean Hamel gets two minutes for playing with an illegal stick, apparently due to its curvature being too wide. It is worth noting that Hamel had spent the past two years in the Nordiques organization playing for head coach Michel Bergeron, save for sixteen games with Quebec's AHL affiliate the Fredericton Express, presumably using a stick with the same illegal dimensions during his time on both teams. 1:17 to go in MTL #17 Ludwig's tripping penalty. Quebec on a five-on-three power play.

00:05:12

QUE #26 Peter Stastny scores a one-timer from a pass by QUE #15 Jean-François Sauvé. Nordiques lead 1–0. 1:49 remaining in Hamel's penalty.

00:09:51

QUE #2 Wally Weir receives a two-minute charging minor after driving MTL #20 Mark Hunter down to the ice from behind. It was Weir's very first shift for the Nordiques after being called up from Fredericton following their elimination from the AHL playoffs.

00:11:58

QUE #25 Blake Wesley gets two minutes for holding after knocking MTL #6 Pierre Mondou to the ice following a frantic sequence in front of the Quebec net started by a rebound from MTL #28 Hamel's slapshot from the point.

00:17:23

QUE #7 Pat Price and MTL #30 Chris Nilan go at each other in the Quebec zone, and each get offsetting minors. Price is penalized for elbowing; Nilan, for slashing. Two minutes apiece.

00:20:00

As the siren sounds the end of the first period, QUE #22, captain Mario Marois, gets called for an elbow against MTL #23, captain Bob Gainey. The Habs will start the second period with a power play.

APPRAISAL

The play has a decent fire-wagon flow to it. Despite being outshot 11 to 8, Quebec looks like the better team. Their passes are clean, whereas Montreal seems frantic and keeps giving the puck away. Most of the action seems to take place in the neutral zone. Guy Lafleur gets momentarily booed by the Forum crowd, but keeps trying to ignite the Montreal offence. Wilf Paiement almost scores a short-handed goal. With the exception of a few robust bodychecks, it is a less chippy period than one might expect, considering the craziness to come. Dale Hunter is all over the ice, and he's making Larry Robinson work for every second of his shift. The goalies look good. Towards the end of the period, there is a mini controversy over referee Bruce Hood not penalizing Montreal's Craig Ludwig for handling the puck. Quebec's head coach, Michel Bergeron, is very angry. His counterpart, Jacques Lemaire, is also less than pleased, but that seems to be down to Montreal not showing up like Quebec has.

SECOND PERIOD
00:03:52
After helping to fight off a fairly aggressive Montreal power play, QUE #16 Goulet bear-hugs MTL #23 Gainey down to the ice; as a result, he gets two minutes for holding. This is Montreal's third power play in a row.

00:09:00 (approx.)
After a rebound from MTL #30 Nilan's slapshot, there is a flurry of action in the Quebec end. MTL #26 Mats Naslund whips a cross-ice pass to MTL #24 Chris Chelios, who hits the post. Nilan pounces on the rebound, and he, too, hits the post.

Much of the Forum crowd thinks it's a goal and cheers prematurely. QUE #22 Marois and Nilan lock sticks in what feels like the prologue to a fight, but they are quickly separated by the officials. Montreal's offence is once again stymied by QUE #35, goalie Dan Bouchard. 1–0 Quebec.

00:15:20

QUE #32 Dale Hunter makes contact with MTL #37, goalie Steve Penney, and is instantly set upon by three different Montreal players including MTL #24 Chelios and Dale's own brother MTL #20 Mark Hunter. Other Nordiques skate in to the rescue and a full-on ruck ensues, each player looking for a dance partner in the wrong jersey. Mark Hunter backs away from his brother and locks arms with QUE #7 Price. There is a noticeable increase in tension and frustration as the officials seem to have a more difficult time separating all the players.

00:17:39

Having just finished serving time for his penalty, QUE #32 Dale Hunter joins QUE #19 Alain Côté on a rush into the Montreal zone. Côté takes a shot from the left wing that is stopped by MTL #37 Penney. Hunter pounces on the rebound, after which MTL #5 Rick Green back-skates into Penney in an attempt to thwart Hunter. Penney, taking exception and apparently mistaking Green's contact with interference on the part of Hunter, proceeds to deck Hunter in the face with his glove hand. Hunter is swarmed by multiple

Canadiens players, including Green. Hunter and Green each get two minutes for roughing. Penney is not penalized.

00:17:59

The puck is thrown back behind the Montreal net and QUE #20 Anton Stastny pounces on it. MTL #17 Ludwig tries to bodycheck Stastny, fails, and the two end up wrestling down to the ice and then back up onto their feet, at which point Ludwig throws a right into Stastny's face and then continues to punch him in the head. Stastny kind of returns fire, and the two eventually get tangled up in a clinch until separated by linesmen Bob Hodges and John D'Amico. Ludwig and Stastny each get five-minute fighting majors.

00:19:44

After maintaining possession in the Quebec end, Montreal cycles offensive positions. As he is making his way past the goal, MTL #24 Chelios is driven into the Quebec net by QUE #24 André Doré. Doré gets two minutes for interference. This is Quebec's fourth penalty in a row. The score is still 1–0 Quebec.

00:19:48

After winning a faceoff in the Quebec end, MTL #15 Smith drops the puck back to the point but keeps his stick locked on QUE #11 André Savard's stick, impeding his ability to move; thus, four seconds into Montreal's fifth power play in a row, they are right back to even strength, as Smith gets two minutes for interference.

00:19:55

With MTL #21 Guy Carbonneau posting up in the Quebec crease, MTL #5 Green tries a slapshot from the point that QUE #35 Bouchard stops. QUE #32 Dale Hunter knocks Carbonneau down to the ice. MTL #24 Chelios pounces on the rebound and takes one last shot right before the siren sounds.

00:20:00

As the siren signals the end of the second frame, MTL #21 Carbonneau is on the ice to the left of the Quebec net, grappling with QUE #32 Dale Hunter. QUE #22 Marois locks sticks with MTL #5 Green. QUE #19 Côté skates in towards Carbonneau and Hunter. MTL #24 Chelios rushes in to help, and that's when it happens: both teams leap from their benches and rush towards the Quebec net, and a donnybrook ensues. Both teams swarm Carbonneau and Hunter, who are still wrestling on the ice. At first, it is just a massive melee—no punches being thrown, just a lot of grabbing of opposite sweaters.

MTL #30 Nilan skates to the back of the ruck and then, for some reason that is hard to ascertain on TV, grabs QUE #21 Randy Moller and starts punching him in the head. Moller drops to the ice. QUE #6 Rick Lapointe notices, stops tussling with Chelios, and turns his attention to Nilan, wrapping his left arm around Nilan's head. MTL #29 John Chabot, who was already trying to hold back Lapointe, then tackles him to the ice, and a pile-on erupts. Chelios tries to grab Lapointe. QUE #30, backup goalie Clint Malarchuk, grabs Chelios.

Malarchuk is then grabbed and spun by MTL #33 Richard Sevigny, the Habs backup for the night.

MTL #35 McPhee makes an attempt to leave the scrum and rush towards the pile-on, presumably to come to Nilan's aid. QUE #25 Wesley tries to impede him, fails, but won't loosen his grasp, and McPhee basically drags him towards the pile-on. MTL #10 Guy Lafleur tries to pull Wesley off McPhee, but is stopped by linesman Hodges.

The scrum dissipates into a bunch of mini scrums. Sevigny and Malarchuk skate to the corner and square up. MTL #14 Mario Tremblay and QUE #26 Peter Stastny lock arms. MTL #11 Ryan Walter and MTL #20 Mark Hunter are in a four-way tug-of-war with QUE #7 Price and some other poor bugger in a blue sweater. MTL #19 Larry Robinson tangos with QUE #27 Paiement. MTL #15 Smith grips jerseys with QUE #9 Tony McKegney. Chabot does the same with QUE #24 Doré.

Dale Hunter and QUE #20 Anton Stastny are back on the Quebec bench.

Referee Bruce Hood stands back.

Tremblay shakes away Peter Stastny's grip, drops his gloves, and starts throwing rights in Stastny's face. McKegney tries to grab Tremblay's sweater, but is prevented by Smith. Stastny tries to punch back at Tremblay, fails, and elects to just clinch him. Tremblay wraps his arm around Stastny's head, and Stastny drives the both of them down to the ice. Doré skates in to help Stastny, but Chabot is still holding him, and the two end up toppling down on top of Stastny and Tremblay.

Sevigny and Malarchuk, each their club's backup for the night, square up and punch each other.

QUE #12 Louis Sleigher and MTL #28 Hamel are tangled up against the glass.

Nilan and Moller get to their feet and exchange blows, and get tied up against the glass. Moller's face is cut and he's bleeding. Linesman Hodges separates them, but Moller keeps trying to get back to Nilan.

Linesman D'Amico tries to separate Sleigher and Hamel. Tremblay skates in to try to pull Sleigher off Hamel. Sleigher frees his left hand and fires it into Hamel's face, dropping him to the ice instantly, where he lays face down. Hamel is motionless. Tremblay drops to his side. Lafleur arrives to join him, both of them trying in vain to rouse Hamel or, at the very least, to ascertain how injured he is. Hamel's fall to the ice seems to serve as something of a whistle, snapping all the on-ice combatants out of their rage. All eyes are on Jean Hamel. D'Amico skates Sleigher back to the dressing room tunnel. MTL #23 Gainey arrives at Hamel's side. Moments later he is joined by Montreal Canadiens trainer Gaétan Lefebvre. The energy has been taken out of the donnybrook, and now all players on the ice are kind of just frozen, still locked onto opposing jerseys but robbed of adrenaline. Players from both teams start to loosen their grasps on one another. Hamel has started to move a little, rolling over onto his left. He is bleeding profusely, his blood visible on the ice. Lefebvre tries to absorb some of it with a rag.

The Nordiques begin to make their way back to their

dressing room, to the sound of boos from the Forum crowd. Lefebvre has managed to get Jean Hamel sitting up against the boards. He is still visibly shaken, and concussed, and doesn't seem to know where he is. Lefebvre is joined by Montreal Canadiens team doctor Douglas Kinnear. Lefebvre and Carbonneau succeed in getting Hamel to his feet. The Forum applauds. Lefebvre and Carbonneau lead Hamel off the ice and back to the Montreal dressing room, flanked by Dr. Kinnear, Lafleur, and Chelios. The rest of Montreal's players follow suit, and the second period is finally over.

APPRAISAL

Montreal comes out at the top of the second with much more ferocity, intention, and discipline than was on display in the first. They have the run of play and generate an embarrassment of offensive opportunities, every single one of them answered and stymied by Bouchard and the Quebec Nordiques defence. The Montreal players seem increasingly frustrated by every chance that goes begging. This frustration is exacerbated by their inability to capitalize on four power plays in a row, and starts manifesting itself in lost tempers. Smith's penalty four seconds into Montreal's last power play seems to be the straw that breaks the camel's back, and shortly thereafter, everything devolves.

One can't help the feeling that the ensuing donnybrook was easily avoidable. With the exception of Sleigher's cheap shot on Hamel, Montreal wins the majority of the tilts but, ultimately, looks the lesser of the two clubs because they're still down a goal, and this whole bench-clearing brawl feels like the lashing-out of a petulant child. Linesmen D'Amico and Hodges do their best to bounce and quell the brawl, while referee Bruce Hood looks shell-shocked and not quite sure how to handle any of it.

THIRD PERIOD

The Nordiques skate out first, followed by the Canadiens, who are greeted with raucous approval from the Forum crowd. The scoreboard is decorated in penalties. From the scoreboard we know that MTL #15 Smith and QUE #24 Doré each have 1:48 and 1:44 respectively left to serve for their interference penalties.

MTL #21 Carbonneau gets a two-minute minor, as does MTL #28 Hamel. It is not apparent why either of them have been chosen, especially Hamel, who was barely conscious as he was escorted back to the Montreal dressing room. QUE #32 Dale Hunter gets a four-minute double minor for roughing.

Bruce Hood stands by the timekeeper, flanked by each team's captain, MTL #23 Gainey and QUE #22 Marois, trying to explain his judicial metric as the Forum announcer, Claude Mouton, starts to officially list off all the penalties doled out for the brawl. It is then that we realize that the data on the scoreboard is only a fraction of the story—there are way more penalties to announce.

QUE #30 Malarchuk gets five minutes for fighting. So does QUE #21 Moller, plus a game misconduct. This last detail elicits a cheer from the Montreal crowd. The next announcement yields an even bigger one, as QUE #26 Peter Stastny is given the same treatment, game misconduct and all. Taking what seems like a great deal of exception to Stastny's penalty, Quebec head coach Bergeron snaps and starts yelling at Hood as Marois skates to the bench, presumably to let Bergeron know what Hood told him and his counterpart, Gainey.

At this point, Moller goes after one of the myriad Canadiens players skating around the ice. Hood rushes in to restrain him at the Quebec blue line. Moller starts giving Hood an earful, and Hood answers by enforcing his penalty and throwing Moller out of the game. Quebec players Doré and McKegney try in vain to persuade Hood to change his mind, while linesman Hodges stands in Moller's way, trying to escort him back to the Quebec dressing room. Moller stops at the Nordiques bench, where Bergeron looks to be trying to calm him down. Moller is apoplectic and threatens to deke away from Hodges' grip and skate into the Canadiens zone. Bergeron grabs Moller's jersey, holding him in place, while he says something angry to Hodges.

The third period still has yet to begin.

Claude Mouton begins to list the penalties incurred by the Canadiens, to the boos of the Forum crowd. MTL #33 Sevigny gets five minutes for fighting. Mouton is in the process of saying *"Le numéro vingt-et-un, Guy Carbonneau—"* when his attention, like everyone else's in the stadium, is interrupted by MTL #20 Mark Hunter dropping his gloves and rushing at

QUE #12 Sleigher, presumably to avenge the wounded Jean Hamel. Led by their captain, Marois, Sleigher's teammates instantly swarm and shield him before Hunter has a chance to get close. Marois, in an apparent effort to prevent another fight from breaking out, turns his back to Hunter while still standing in his way. Nordiques players keep skating in, as do the Canadiens, and another scrum starts to form. QUE #15 Sauvé tries to pry Hunter away from Marois.

MTL #35 McPhee and QUE #2 Weir exchange some pleasantries, and then McPhee rushes Weir. McKegney tries to pull McPhee away, to no avail. McPhee and Weir lock onto each other's cuffs for a few seconds before McPhee shakes his right free and throws it into Weir's face. The Forum roars. On the CBC, Bob Cole voices lament and abhorrence, crying out, "Ahh, here she goes again," and you can almost hear his head shaking at the end of it. Weir manages to parry McPhee's next punch, but fails to meet the punch after that. Weir throws a right that connects with the top of McPhee's helmet, likely hurting himself more than he hurt McPhee, and he elects to grab hold of McPhee's arms and spin before wrestling him down to the ice. Bob Hodges skates in to separate them. McPhee and Weir maintain very tense grips on each other, likely swearing the whole time.

For some reason, Dale Hunter and Canadiens backup goalie Richard Sevigny try to fight each other. This is quickly ended by the arrival of MTL #29 Chabot and MTL #24 Chelios, as well as Malarchuk. Malarchuk grabs hold of Sevigny, and Sevigny answers in kind. Chabot looks like he wants to get into a fight with Hunter, whereas Chelios seems to want to prevent another one from happening.

The Canadiens head coach, Jacques Lemaire, physically restrains Carbonneau at the Montreal bench, "trying" as Bob Cole put it, "to get some sense into this . . . situation here." And aside from McPhee and Weir's grappling session on the ice, it seems as if the donnybrook is dissipating.

Claude Mouton is in the process of letting the audience know that MTL #30 Nilan has two different five-minute fighting penalties to serve, a ten-minute misconduct, and a game misconduct, when Mark Hunter swings his stick at Sleigher. Sleigher dodges it and is instantly protected by teammates, who pry Hunter's stick away from him. The Forum crowd erupts, and the brawl seems to be flaring right back up again.

Sevigny lunges at Dale Hunter and starts punching him in the head. Hunter returns fire. Malarchuk skates in and smothers Sevigny, trying to pull him off Hunter. Carbonneau arrives and grabs hold of Malarchuk's sweater. Doré grabs Carbonneau's sweater, and in an instant, the ice is covered in a tangled mass of angry hockey players.

Mouton continues listing Montreal's penalties. One can't help feeling like this is an effort to force a bit of normality onto what is clearly a very abnormal situation. MTL #14 Tremblay gets five minutes for fighting, a ten-minute misconduct, and a game misconduct. As this is being announced, Tremblay looks to be trying to get at Sleigher, but is prevented from doing so by QUE #16 Goulet. Tremblay keeps trying to break free of Goulet's grasp, but Goulet holds firm, and they just sort of skate around in a weird mass that has snowballed to include MTL #22 Steve Shutt, Sleigher, and an unidentifiable Quebec player.

And then, over the PA system, comes the last of Montreal's penalties: MTL #28 Hamel, two minutes for unsportsmanlike conduct. Presumably for being sucker-punched unconscious. The announcement of this penalty is met by boos from the Montreal crowd.

Once again the scrum dissipates, and both teams start to separate as Bruce Hood tries to get them all back to their respective locker rooms.

Mark Hunter then darts away from his teammates and makes a beeline for Sleigher. Mark's brother Dale moves to stop him. Mark jukes and grabs hold of Dale's sweater for a few moments before letting go to run at Sleigher. Dale is about to stop him when Tremblay leaps in from behind and tackles Dale to the ice. In a flash, Doré is on Tremblay, feeding him a flurry of heavy punches. Carbonneau makes a break to rescue Tremblay, but is yanked backwards and spun away by QUE #19 Côté. McKegney is there too, trying to pull Dale Hunter out of the pile. The Forum crowd is going insane.

Goulet gets between Mark Hunter and Sleigher and, putting his own teammate in a headlock, forces Sleigher back to the dressing room.

Before long, a crowd develops around the Hunter-Tremblay-Doré pile, every player trying to prevent their opponents from adding to the mayhem. Sevigny gets close and starts trying to pull Doré off Tremblay. Malarchuk skates in to pull Sevigny off Doré. For a few fleeting moments, it feels as if the worst might be over. And then Peter Stastny skates in and starts punching Tremblay, who, face down at the bottom of the pile, can do nothing but get punched. MTL #10 Lafleur pulls Stastny away and is then restrained by Sauvé.

The crowd starts fragmenting into clusters of opposing players. Whilst being pulled in opposite directions, Tremblay and Dale Hunter manage to get to their feet. Hunter starts punching Tremblay for a few moments before his brother Mark comes flying in and tackles both of them to the ice.

For reasons that are still unclear, Sevigny is once again trying to get at Dale Hunter, and once again he is neutralized by Malarchuk. Malarchuk eventually finds a way to put Sevigny in a headlock that Sevigny easily frees himself from. Both men look very tired and just sort of drift backwards to the boards. Neither of them will let go of his opponent.

With the help of players from both teams, Bob Hodges finally manages to separate Tremblay, Dale Hunter, and Mark Hunter. And as the Forum crowd belts out the familiar tune of "Na-na-na-na, hey-hey-hey, goodbye," all three are sent to their dressing rooms.

Claude Mouton begins listing all of the penalties in English.

All players still on the ice are congregating around the time-keeper, presumably trying to sort through who got penalized for what offence. Everyone looks exhausted and ready for this to be done. The ice is littered with sticks, helmets, and gloves, like shrapnel and weapons after corpses have been removed from a battlefield. There is a sincere feeling of calm. Not peace, calm. As if everyone agrees that a moment's respite is required. As if everyone knows they are past the violent, tragic narrative low point at the end of the second act, and are ready for the third to begin. The players all take their usual spots on their respective benches, and the starting lines for each team skate around the ice like they would at the start of any other period. They, too, seem intent on forcing normality onto an abnormal situation. And they succeed.

00:00:00

The period begins with a three-on-three, due to the minors given to MTL #15 Smith, QUE #24 Doré, MTL #21 Carbonneau, and MTL #28 Hamel, who has still not returned from the Montreal dressing room, as well as a double minor for roughing given to QUE #32 Dale Hunter, even though Hunter himself has been banished with a game misconduct.

The game misconducts have taken their toll on both teams, as evidenced by the gaping holes on each bench. Quebec Nordiques Peter Stastny, Louis Sleigher, Dale Hunter, Clint Malarchuk, and Wally Weir, as well as Montreal Canadiens Chris Nilan, Mario Tremblay, Mark Hunter, Mike McPhee, and Richard Sevigny have all been sent home for the night. Quebec and Montreal have each been reduced to just fifteen players in uniform.

MTL #19 Robinson, flanked by MTL #6 Mondou, skates

out for the faceoff with MTL #24 Chelios bringing up the rear. QUE #22 Marois, QUE #11 Savard, and QUE #6 Lapointe skate in to meet them at centre ice. Savard wins the faceoff and, with Quebec still nursing a tenuous one-goal lead, the third period finally begins.

00:02:02

With just one or possibly two seconds remaining in a four-second-long four-on-three advantage, Quebec adds to their lead. To the right of the Montreal net, MTL #19 Robinson tries to clear the puck and ends up just gifting it to QUE #16 Goulet, who easily backhands it through MTL #37 Penney's legs. 2–0 Quebec.

00:06:23

Flanked by two Nordiques in the neutral zone, MTL #15 Smith feeds a cross-ice pass to MTL #22 Shutt. QUE #18 Marian Stastny and QUE #24 Doré try in vain to stop Shutt, who opens up on QUE #35 Bouchard's glove side from a distance and scores. 2–1 Quebec.

00:06:46

The puck squirts away to the side of the Montreal net. MTL #23 Gainey pounces on it. QUE #16 Goulet, who added to Quebec's tally just moments ago, is on Gainey almost immediately. After narrowly avoiding taking a high-sticking penalty, Goulet takes Gainey's legs out from under him and gets two minutes for tripping.

00:09:11

Less than thirty seconds after the teams are back to even strength, MTL #26 Naslund carries the puck back into the Quebec zone, and after enduring a hit against the boards, sneaks the puck to MTL #22 Shutt from behind the Quebec net. QUE #35 Bouchard looks to his right, presumably tracking Naslund and anticipating a wrap-around attempt. Shutt one-times the puck past Bouchard's stick and into the back of the net. Quebec and Montreal are now tied up, at two goals apiece. There is a palpable shift of momentum in Montreal's favour. The Forum crowd explodes into cheers. The stadium is filled with chants of "Go Habs Go!"

00:12:14

MTL #15 Smith carries the puck into the Quebec zone and gets it across the blue line to MTL #5 Green. Green wastes no time and rockets a heavy slapshot into the top left corner of the Quebec net. 3–2 Montreal.

00:13:27

Just over a minute later, MTL #26 Naslund pounces on the puck to the right of the Quebec net and almost instantly feeds it to MTL #10 Lafleur, who hovers, wide open, in front of QUE #35 Bouchard. Lafleur fans on the puck, but it is very quickly picked up by MTL #29 Chabot. Chabot plays with the puck for a few seconds before backhanding it across the goal mouth and into the back of the net. 4–2 Montreal.

The Forum crowd is at what feels like a fever pitch. On the CBC, Bob Cole and Mickey Redmond remark that this is the loudest the Forum has been in years. The chorus of "Na-na-na-na" picks up again. This time it's in earnest, and it rings out through the whole building.

00:14:28

MTL #11 Walter feeds an outlet pass up-ice to MTL #21 Carbonneau, who carries it into the Quebec zone with MTL #23 Gainey to his left on a two-on-one breakaway. Carbonneau opts to try his luck and goes glove side on QUE #35 Bouchard with a gentle wrist shot (which may very well have been an attempted pass) that slides through Bouchard's legs into the back of the net. This is Montreal's fifth straight unanswered goal. 5–2 Montreal.

00:16:51

QUE #15 Sauvé drops the puck back to QUE #27 Paiement, who fires a howitzer that MTL #37 Penney is helpless to stop. The Forum crowd stops singing. 5–3 Montreal.

End of game.

Final score: Montreal Canadiens 5, Quebec Nordiques 3.

APPRAISAL

It is difficult to avoid placing at least some of the blame for the brawl on Louis Sleigher. Of course the game was chippy and the Canadiens were frustrated and ready to snap. Of course everything had an edge to it; of course the brawl had already broken out by the time Sleigher cheap-shotted Jean Hamel in the face. But once he did, what could have fizzled out burned brighter than ever, and careers were changed by it. The Canadiens would win the series that night, thereby putting an end to Quebec's season. Bruce Hood would eventually be forced to retire. Jean Hamel would never play another NHL game in his life; his career ended with the Sleigher cheap shot. He never returned to the ice during game 6, nor did he play in any of the games against the Islanders in the following round. He would make an appearance at the Canadiens camp in the summer, but he ultimately opted to retire altogether.

It was a significant, awful moment, in a game full of them. Did Louis Sleigher know that he would knock Hamel unconscious, thereby sending him face-first to the ice, where his face would split open? Probably not. Did Louis Sleigher know exactly what he was doing? Probably. He is by no means the cause of the evening's violence, but he played a significant role in it, and his actions prolonged it.

It is equally difficult not to lay blame on Bruce Hood. He lost control of his hockey game, and he displayed almost no calm under pressure. When shit hit the fan, he folded; he let the fights run their course, and in so doing forfeited his right to adjudicate the game. He missed every opportunity to calm things down, and he left his linesmen to fend for themselves. He let the players regulate each other and made himself irrelevant in the process. This seems to have occurred to him at some point during the second intermission, as his handing out of penalties seems almost random or irrational.

The two-minute minor penalty for unsportsmanlike conduct he issues to Jean Hamel, for instance. Or the fact that, while both Hunters and Peter Stastny get game misconducts, Mario Tremblay and André Doré are allowed to keep playing in the third period. None of it really makes any sense.

Once the third period actually begins, the play is self-conscious, both teams firmly stuck in their respective heads. The donnybrooks' impact is palpable, but it is still unclear who, if anyone, will shift the momentum to their advantage. At first, it seems like Quebec has done so, and they get another goal for their efforts. This advantage is fleeting and short-lived, and the Canadiens quickly come to life. They're back in the fight with their first goal, and threaten a whirlwind with their second. The third and fourth goals lift the Canadiens to a discernible dominance, which is confirmed by the fifth. It feels like a different game. Somehow, it already feels over and done with for Quebec. The Canadiens have dominated the run of play and dictated the period's momentum. The brawls seem to have energized them, and yet also seem long ago.

Quebec threatens revenge with Paiement's goal at 16:51. All of a sudden the tension and drama of the evening's events seem vital and relevant once again, and the game seems like it could still be up for grabs. For a few moments, the deficit stops feeling insurmountable. But ultimately, the fates have chosen their winners, and everyone in the Forum seems to know who they are.

The Canadiens would go on to face the New York Islanders in the next round, eventually losing that series four games to two.

In the rear-view, with the benefit of hindsight and the patina of romance, this game has taken on a sort of mythic status, and it's easy to forget that all of the drama was very much avoidable. One or two different decisions by the officials, and this game would have been like any other game 6: exciting, tenacious, chintzy, edgy, but still a hockey game. Which is how this particular game 6 started off and eventually finished. But in the midst of the twenty-minute stanza of violence and disorder, one feels like this is all it ever was and all it would ever be: two gangs in a tit-for-tat blood feud. Any event born of revenge begs a sort of "chicken or egg" question, but at a certain point, causation is irrelevant, because as Gandhi said, "An eye for an eye makes the whole world go blind."

However, it would be disingenuous of me to pretend that I wasn't captivated by every second of it.

There are reasons I have written a timeline for this game, of all the hockey games the Montreal Canadiens have ever played. What happened that night at the Forum was uncommon, and staggering, and the world of hockey remembers it to this day. Sure, much of the fascination for it may be like that of a car crash. Much of it might appeal to a base blood lust that I, like many people, possess and make efforts to mitigate. But I believe the reason I find this game so compelling, the reason it has taken on and maintained a certain poetry, which it was gilded with the very second the third period drew to a close, is that it was a pure rendering of the relevant themes of the night, and of all of team sport: tribalism and competition. It was ugly and cynical and immature, and so is every other game in which a bunch of people in one set of colours compete against another bunch of people in a different set of colours.

Maybe the Good Friday Massacre just cut a little too close to the bone.

Game 6 didn't need to, and shouldn't have had to, play out the way it did, but very few games of the modern era have been half as compelling to watch.

TWENTY-FIVE

IN THE SUMMER of 2017, the NHL got a bit fatter. Gary Bettman and his cabal of loyalists and puppet owners of failed franchises, in all of their infinite wisdom, finally rolled up their sleeves and gave the world something it didn't seem to need: a professional hockey team in Las Vegas, complete with a team name as hokey as it is abstract: the Golden Knights. I am familiar with the words *golden* and *knights*, but really don't know what this specific pairing is in reference to, nor what it has to do with Las Vegas. Regardless, the Golden Knights are now a thing, and the league is that much more logjammed, and the Habs have that much less of a shot at winning the Cup, and our chances of drafting quality players have dropped that much more.

All of this is made even more depressing by the fact that the Las Vegas Golden Knights started their history by making it all the way to the fucking Stanley Cup finals in the spring of 2018. They already have a better shot at winning the Stanley Cup than the Habs. Just like all the other teams in the league. They all seem to be possessed of the same advantage of not being us, of not being so singularly obsessed with where we used to be. In lieu of history and tradition, the Golden Knights have pyrotechnics and the tone-deaf use of clips from *Apocalypse Now*. And being free from the weight of the obligations of history and emotion, the Golden Knights were able to fight their way to a Stanley Cup final in the first year of their existence. Which is unprecedented in NHL history, and massively depressing. But good on them. Because their gaudy, deconstructed version of our game is the epitome of everything that we, as Habs fans, think we are better than, and the success of the Golden Knights proves that we aren't. We haven't been better than anything or anyone for a very long time.

Like any team with history, the Montreal Canadiens place an importance on certain numbers. There are the jersey numbers, once stitched to the backs of Habs icons, preserved for eternal reverence on the ceiling of the Bell Centre. Numbers like 9 and 4 and 33. Numbers that instantly trigger wellsprings of sentiment in any Habs fans. These are numbers that are forever linked to surnames like Richard and Béliveau and Roy, an enduring reward for their efforts and contributions to Habs mythos, and no Habs player can ever use them again. We hear them or read them, and we are afforded instant context. Just as when we hear or read numbers like '93 or '86 or '77 or 1909, we feel an instant reverence for years that are almost as important and vital to us as the year we were born. We know and honour these years because they were our best, and they are surely behind us. We have victories—important victories of the highest competitive order—and like medieval monarchs and knights who name their greatest military successes after their location, we name our Cups by the year we won them.

We celebrate the past and honour these numbers because we are unhappy with the present and all but completely crippled by another number. This is a number unlike the others, as it is not a reference to something that has happened, but to something that has yet to occur. It is a reminder of our generation-long stasis, and the name of an alluring treasure we will spend our lives in pursuit of. It is an odd number that feels even, and until we possess it, until we can call it ours, it will taunt us and drive us mad.

The number is twenty-five, and it is the name of the Cup we've yet to win. Twenty-five is a siren, beautiful and aspirational; the sum total of desire. Twenty-five is also addictive, and possessive, and it caters to everything ugly inside of us. Twenty-five is the Stanley Cup that never came home. Twenty-five is the name of the drought and the famine that has plagued not only Montreal, but all of Canada, since 1993. Twenty-five is the Grail, and twenty-five is the Ring. The closest thing we have to twenty-five is twenty-four; they are similar but very different. Twenty-four is a reminder of everything good we've done, while also being a reminder of everything we can never do. Twenty-four consoles us, while twenty-five taunts us. For more than twenty-five years, the Cup has been away from home, and no Habs fan will ever sleep totally soundly until it returns. We need it, and the need is killing us.

When the knights of King Arthur's Round Table had their collective vision of the Holy Grail, they all knew that the rest of their lives would be devoted to that quest. It was a quest as allegorical and rhetorical as it was literal, and the harder they sought the Grail, the further from it they seemed. King Arthur and Britain, meanwhile, grew sick and fell into disorder, Camelot reduced to a museum of old victories. The longer the quest endured, the longer Arthur's knights were away from home, the sicker and weaker the land and its king became. The land was without its Cup, and life was worse because of it. It was not a mere vanity, but an elemental life force intrinsically connected to a land and its people. They needed it, and the need was killing them.

Any Habs fan is also a philosopher. Not by choice, but by necessity. To be inundated with so much imagery and history and ceremony, and yet to be constantly disappointed by a lot of actual hockey, is to be forced to try to reconcile it all. How is it that the team I love and watch through eighty-two frustrating games a season is the same team we honour with twenty minutes of pregame history-lesson movies? How is it that I feel superior and entitled by vintage, born into less a fandom than a religion, and yet our lions are middling? Why the fuck can't we just be awesome again and win our twenty-fifth Stanley Cup?

If Habs fans are philosophers, then this is the ultimate question, the very apex of hockey existentialism, the single

intellectual problem we all devote the most time to. Everything is an extension of that question. Every furrowed brow,
angry blog post, hugged stranger, and cherished moment—it
all comes back to the Cup. Every happy thing is a mini version of winning it and a stepping stone on the path towards
it. Every unhappy thing is a symptom of all that's keeping us
from becoming what we're supposed to be: daring, and bold,
and inspiring, and intimidating. Everything we used to be,
everything that seems a generation or two away.

So what the fuck happened? Why have we lost our mojo
in such a profound way? How did we turn from centrepiece
to wallpaper, from life of the party to weird guy at the bar?
When did the decline begin, and when will it end, if ever?
Why can't the Montreal Canadiens win another Stanley Cup?

There are many reasons for this, the biggest one being
that the Stanley Cup is the hardest trophy to win in professional sports, coming at the end of what is clearly an over-
long eighty-two-game regular season, as well as almost two
months of gruelling post-season. There are thirty other teams
with the same ambition standing between us and the championship. This is also a very different NHL than the one we
conquered in 1993. The league is bigger than it was even a
decade ago, let alone when the Habs were relevant, and more
teams means fewer quality players to choose from, and the
NHL still plays their games on ice surfaces with dimensions
agreed upon during the Depression, but the boys are bigger,
faster, and covered in more padding than ever before. There
is far less fighting, yes, but far more potentially career-ending

head injuries due to cheap shots and open-ice collisions. NHL goaltenders are wider and taller than they've ever been, and their pads cover more daylight than Patrick Roy's did. They also reap the advantages of competing in an era where every game has a winner. The last time we won the championship, it was a hard-fought honour for surviving a season where every game had three potential outcomes, as opposed to the binary options available now. The play is more frenetic than before, and somehow more tentative as well. Players seem to shoot less than they once did, and the Habs haven't had a fifty-goal scorer since Stephane Richer. And even if the likes of Ovechkin do hit the fifty-goal mark season in and season out, we all know we will likely never see numbers like Gretzky's or Lemieux's, or rookie seasons like Teemu Selänne's, ever again. The game itself is different. It is an offshoot, a distillation of the game we used to play. The old game. We were champions of the old game. We are faceless competitors in the new game, stock opponents for the real stars to best en route to glory.

NHL hockey is different and, dare I say, also more boring than it used to be. God bless the Montreal Canadiens, and God bless the Original Six, and God bless the first wave of expansion teams, but holy fuck are we saturated now. What we have before us, as hockey fans in the modern era, is an overly defensive, whitewashed, Americanized version of the best game you can name.

Filtered through the unpleasantness and chaos of four different work stoppages in thirty years, and synthesized beyond recognition in an effort to appeal to as many new fans as possible, modern-era NHL hockey is the pro sports equivalent of a gentrified neighbourhood. There's more money, and there's been an aesthetic shift from folksy and provincial to slick and global, and it has all come at the cost of sincerity and tradition. The NHL moved its heart from Toronto to New York, and with it went a lot of what made hockey hockey. The Prince of Wales and Campbell conferences became the Eastern and Western conferences, and hot-weather places were given hockey teams, for some reason, one of which was named after a fucking Disney movie. It's like the NHL saw what Giuliani did to Manhattan and Pol Pot did to Phnom Penh and was like, "Yup, that's what should happen to hockey." They fixed something that wasn't broken, and real hockey fans have been paying the price ever since.

Or at least Habs fans have. Or maybe we haven't. Maybe we just haven't been good enough, and I should temper my expectations. Maybe this is all just old-fart syndrome, nostalgia for a time I don't really remember. Maybe it's just evolution and, though scoring is down, other things are up. Maybe the league isn't bloated, and if I'm truly a hockey fan, I should really just be psyched, if anything, because more teams means more hockey.

But I don't think it's as simple as us being out of date; it's not just that the game changed but we didn't. I think we changed too, just maybe not for the better. Like monarchs of once-powerful kingdoms, now reduced to pomp and ceremony and legacy alone, the Habs have been in an existential tailspin since 1993. Over time, our old reputation faded and joined the pages of history, while our present looked less and less flattering. We have not only scrambled to keep up with our competitors and the hockey world itself, but we have also found ourselves caught between huge decade-sized rocks and hard places. As the rest of the league looked to the future, we have only ever looked behind us, or down at our skates. The league changed, and changed again, ever evolving. What's required to win it all now is not the same as it was the last time we won. There is a constantly shifting list of requirements for championship, and we have yet to meet all of them at any one point.

There are also advantages we once possessed that we no longer do. Namely financial ones. It's not that we are losing money, or aren't as profitable as we once were, it's that we've been cut off at the knees so that hockey may be brought to all the people in the desert who weren't asking for it. As with any industry, in hockey, some teams, like the Montreal Canadiens, make more money than other teams. The teams that make more money, like the Montreal Canadiens, do so because they have a more dedicated fan base than the others, and yet, instead of being rewarded for our dedication, for buying tickets and merch, or paying for a cable package of forty channels just so we can watch RDS or TSN or Sportsnet, we fans are punished and our team is hindered by the existence of the salary cap.

I would assume any person or group of persons with enough resources to own an NHL team must be fairly ardent capitalists to get where they've gotten. Competition and the laissez-faire free market allowed them to make their money, and yet they cry parity and encode a lack of responsibility in some sort of civic-minded "for the good of the game" nonsense. They peddle a product in a market where people have no appetite for it, and instead of taking their licks and closing up shop, they persist, and double down, and shirk their debt onto the shoulders of city councils. They demand fairness and equality, and the Habs are hindered by the existence of the Arizona Coyotes. We have resources that we can't spend because no one in Glendale wants to watch hockey.

Money is not a guarantee of success, as any Manchester City fan will tell you, but it definitely fucking helps. Especially in a place like Montreal, with its high taxes, subarctic living conditions, and the impossibility of anonymity for anyone who plays for the Habs. Teams like the Habs and the Leafs have to work that much harder to convince free agents to come play for them, and it would be nice to know that we could've won the Kovalchuk sweepstakes by just throwing an obscene amount of money at him for one season. We'd have been able to. We and the Leafs and the Rangers are constantly ranked in the top three in terms of financial success, and yet none of us has won a championship in a generation. All because the Bettman experiment, with all of its pandering and hubris and looking of Canadian hockey fan gift horses in the mouth, cannot be allowed to fail. It is a product of that most American of conditions, financial hypocrisy. It's "all is fair in love and war" until the rich start hemorrhaging money, and then it's "too big to fail" and bullshit egalitarianism.

It is especially frustrating for those of us who support teams that existed before the league itself did. The Montreal Canadiens were born in 1909, and the NHL is nothing more than the stiffs who allow us to play against other teams. We were around before them, and should the NHL ever collapse completely, I'd like to think we'd still be around long after them. And there are many times throughout a season when that becomes a real pipe dream, and I wonder how much better off we'd be as an organization if we didn't play in the NHL.

But we do. And have done since the league's inception. This is where we have won all of our greatest victories, and if we are to compete against the best in the world, the NHL is the only show in town. And being a Canadian hockey fan, one can't help but feel that the NHL really doesn't want a Canadian champion. There have been twenty-four Stanley Cup finals between 1993 and 2018, and only five have featured a Canadian team: Vancouver in '94 and '11, Calgary in '04, Edmonton in '06, and Ottawa in '07, each of them ultimately going home empty-handed. Some come very close, as the Flames did against Tampa Bay, only to have their hearts shattered in a final that was controversial, to say the least.

Every year, different pockets of Canadian hockey fans hold their collective breath, hoping that this might be the year their city gets an NHL team. Every year, citizens of Quebec City, the GTA, and the Maritimes all trick themselves into believing the pipe dream that the NHL wants them to believe: that they are valued, and if they just keep the faith long enough, they will be rewarded. Of course this never happens, because Gary Bettman loves sand and takes Canada for granted, and vulgar displays of wealth are more important than logic or reason— neither of which would dictate putting a hockey team in the live-entertainment capital of the world, which also happens to be in the arse end of the fucking desert. Regardless of the fact that Quebec City has a brand-new, multi-million-dollar, state-of-the-art hockey stadium and a local fan base full of antipathy towards Montreal.

There are more NHL teams in hot-weather climates than there are in all of Canada. In a league of thirty-one teams, only seven are located in the country that gave birth to hockey, and raised it, and held it aloft as our living art, defining lives and our collective consciousness since its inception. We came up with it, and nothing has come close to matching the connection we, as a country, have to this sport. We are under-represented and outnumbered in the association of athletic clubs we began, and yet we are overrepresented in the work-force that actually makes up the league. We have one-tenth the population of the United States, yet we make up close to half the league's players. Once upon a time, we could claim 75 percent of them, though that number has been in decline since the 1980s. Still, the vast majority of NHL coaches, general managers, scouts, referees, and linesmen are born of the True North strong and free. In attendance numbers, Canadian teams are constantly in the top ten. But none of that matters, because the NHL sold its soul, and potential American customers who have yet to be poached are far more important than the loyal, dyed-in-the-wool Canadian fan base the league has relied on for years. Is it a coincidence that 1993, the last time we won the Cup, also happened to be the first season of the Anaheim Mighty Ducks' existence? We remain the last Canadian team to win the Stanley Cup, as if the NHL knew it was about to sell its soul and let its oldest franchise have one last kick at the can before unleashing generation Bettman. It was as if they allowed our country one last honour before appropriating our art form, potentially forever. Part of me (a very small, almost imperceptible part of me) envies the "fans" of the Las Vegas Golden Knights, because as phony and new and pointless as their team might be, whatever happens to them is gravy. The team cannot shame themselves, or choke, or disappoint, or fall short of expectations. Because there are no expectations; there is only a blank slate, a history being written. They have nothing to lose, and therefore have a degree of invincibility, and possibly even more of a chance of winning. At the very least, they have the freedom to be bold, to take risks, to aim for the skies or die trying. They aren't constantly drowning under the weight of their own legacy, as we are. Any post-season presence at all is a success. Any post-season success the Habs might have will be seen as overachievement in the context of the season, but underachievement in the context of all of Habs history.

We can never be as good as we used to be. So maybe that shouldn't be our goal. Maybe our goal should be to be better than we used to be. Maybe we need to be different, changed in the right kind of way. Maybe we need to be new. Maybe we need to pretend there aren't twenty-four championships behind us. Maybe we need to pretend that we've never won a championship before. Maybe we should shut our mouths and stop referencing our past every time someone shits on our present. Maybe we need to burn our history and kill our romance—or, at least, ignore them. Maybe we should pretend there was no Guy Lafleur, no Rocket Richard, no Jean Béliveau, no Patrick Roy, no Forum, no such thing as a dynasty. Maybe the only way for us to compete in the modern-era NHL is to act like we just got here. Maybe we don't start all forty-one home games with prolonged Jumbotron odes to everything we used to be. Maybe we take down our banners and leave our ceiling bare. Maybe we need to forget about where we came from and care only about what's in front of us. Maybe it's time for us to step outside of our bubble and abandon any sense of entitlement we have. Maybe we are at the point in our hero's journey where we have to fuck off to the woods and forget ourselves while we find ourselves. Maybe it's time for our hero to look into his past and do the hard work of severing ties. Maybe it's time to *let go*. Maybe it's time for us to triage our priorities and acknowledge that so long as the Habs are more than just a hockey team, we will always be at an inherent disadvantage. Maybe it's time for us to ask ourselves what's more important, our history or our future? Maybe it's time for us to redefine what it means to be the Habs. Maybe.

But I know, as any Habs fan knows, that to do any of that, to purge our team of its patrimony and its transcendence,

would be robbing us of everything we know and take ownership of. We need that otherness, that romance, that institutional refusal to evolve; without these elements, the Habs
would cease to be the Habs and would become the Senators,
or any other team whose fan base takes their cultural cues
from us. We would become just another hockey team, desperately trying to write its own history, with no concerns other
than filling its empty trophy case.

It is a blessing, and a curse, to be the originators of something special, to make up the rank and file of the old guard, to
participate in traditions others seek to emulate.

But it is impossible to successfully move forward if you are
stuck looking behind.

ONE OF THESE SATURDAYS

One of these Saturdays
None of us will
Be alone

And all the ghosts
With their gilt
And overdose guns

Will finish the grey turn
The slow, aching turn
From black to grey
And grey to white

Nothing will be the name
Of the place we used to live
And forgotten will be the blood,
Dissected will be the bones

For there is little more inspiring
Than being in a place together
Where once you were both alone

00:20:00

THIRD PERIOD

THIS IS HOW it ends. It smells like dog shit outside as Canada begins to thaw. Snow-packed boots, red faces, and hunched-up shoulders have been replaced by damp sneakers, overworn hoodies and flannels, and hay fever. We are at home, in my old living room, or standing fast alongside 21,273 other parishioners at the Bell Centre, or in my new house in Toronto. Soon it will be summer and the streets will all smell like BBQ. Hockey season is almost over. Winter's city is going on vacation. It's last call for true Montreal, and everything has led to this final twenty minutes. The night is not young or fresh; we have been here all year. We are down a goal heading into the third.

The city has awoken from its slumber, and the populace is connected in a different way. It seems like every citizen is that much more patient and relaxed; the whole city is lighter. Because a few degrees above zero is reason enough for Montrealers to start eating outside again. Is it actually warm enough for visible calf muscles? No, of course not. But that's hardly the point. Because aside from the fact that six months of −20 makes anything even slightly warmer feel like Tunisia, Montreal wills summer into existence, even if the first six weeks of it are really just spring. The masquerade is worth the effort. Because there is no place like Montreal in the summertime. Humidity and terraces and festivals that bleed into one another like one big two-month-long bender. This is not Montreal at her truest, but it is her at her most vital. In the summer, Montreal lives and loves, and cares little for the consequences. In the summer, Montreal joins the rest of the world.

Not tonight, though. Tonight we are all frozen in a collective inhale, our cynicism replaced by a childlike sense of anticipation. And fear. Lots of fear. It's the last game of the regular season, and as ever, we dangle on the twin precipices of defeat and victory. Everything has led to this moment. And yet, even if we win, though we will celebrate and try our best to carry our elation with us, we know there will be no relief. There can be none. Because a win would only mean we have to keep winning.

We are hoping to come crashing into eighth place, our berth the clumsy, handmade reward for getting hot at the only time you really need to get hot, which is in the final third of the season. It seems like we are forever fighting to stay in the playoff bubble, the eighth and final ticket to the big show the apparent extent of our ambitions. There is no expectation of dominance, like our fathers had for their Habs. All we have is the knowledge that we can't take anything for granted and we don't deserve anything better than the last possible buy-in to the post-season. We get our shit together for the final third, and then ride momentum for as long as we can. There is no confidence. There are no guarantees. There are pins and needles.

I moved to Toronto three years ago. I moved here for a combination of reasons, few of which have any place in this book. I mention it now only because I can feel age and destiny running their courses. I can feel time lapping over me, and I know that chances are I will live here for the rest of my life. Chances are this is where my children will grow up, if and when I have children. I have a good life here. It is not a new life but a continuation and evolution of the one I led in Montreal. This is my home now. A significant portion of my closest friends from back home all seemed to end up here within a decade of each other. I have family here. I have also forged some of the most meaningful friendships in my life since moving here. And when we are all together, my living room here is both my old place in Montreal and Ricky's consulate/apartment in LA. It is home and away, at the same time. It is sovereign Habs soil in the heart of Leafs Nation, and the sum total of every place I've ever enjoyed living.

Everyone is here with me. Amir is here, and so is Evan. And Jesse. And Jacob. And Ricky. And my mum. There are more folks here too. People whose lives have become interwoven with ours. Relatively new faces. Like my buddy George, whom I've known for seven years that feel like thirty in the best way possible. Maybe it's his first-generation Macedonian immigrant common sense, or the fact that he reminds me of the good bits about my dad. Or maybe it's that, even though he's a Scarborough lad through and through, he's more fucking Montreal than a lot of actual Montréalais I know. It's all of this shit and more, and we've been best friends since the word go.

Lauren is here. At the time of this writing, she is my assistant, but she will be my boss eventually. She is smarter, funnier, and wa-a-ay more well adjusted than I was at her age. She has become a little sister to all of us.

Wade is here. So are Andrew and Jason. One of the clearest signs that I am no longer living in Quebec is that I am friends with a dude named Wade. Andrew and Jason are both Scotia boys, and Wade is St. Catharines, Ontario, as fuck. We all made a movie together, and that can be a bond as strong as any shared academic experience. That doesn't mean every time people work on a flick together, they've made friends for life. It just means that sometimes, if the right mix of personalities are thrown together via necessity, and you all enjoy each other's company equally, a movie can vulcanize friendship and you will all keep hanging out long after the flick is done.

Cliff is here. Cliff is my stepdad, though that word feels like treason. Because he is much more than that. He is more my family than a lot of folks I share blood with. He has been a part of my family for a decade, but it feels like he's always been there. In many ways, he is more of a father to me than my dad ever was.

Dad is here too. So is Grandad. And Grandmother. They are watching and feeling and sharing in this moment. They are with me in every moment, but some more than others. Like this one. They are with me. They are watching hockey with me. So is Rocket Richard. And Toe Blake. And Jean Béliveau. So is Ken Dryden. And Guy Lafleur. And Larry Robinson. And Chris Nilan. Bob Gainey is here. Patrick Roy too. Mario Lemieux, Doug Gilmour, and Wendel Clark are all here. So is nineteen-year-old Oshawa General Eric Lindros. And twenty-something John Kordic, who high-fived me from a pay phone when I was four. Kovalev is here, telling me to stop hailing him from my knees like Wayne and Garth. For some reason, Elvis Stojko is here, doing triple axels and hectoring me to "get the jump on taste." Guillaume Latendresse is here, shushing me for singing the national anthem too loudly.

There's a dude who came up to me after a screening of *Goon 2* and told me that they were his favourite movies, that he had gotten married and had a baby in between the first and second flick, that he felt like we'd made those movies for him. He's here.

Rebecca is here too. She is tall, and the most beautiful girl in the world, and nice as fuck, even by Canadian standards. She is the love of my life, despite the distinct disadvantage of having been raised in a family of Leafs fans. In all fairness, she really couldn't care less about any sport, but she likes chirping me. She's the kindest person I've ever known, and I am a better man for being with her. She's here.

The chit-chat dies down and a weighted hush falls upon us. For those of us who are Habs fans, this is it; the roller coaster has not only started its ascent, it has gone through like three loops, and the end is in sight. We feel it in the pit of our stomachs. For the rest of the room, the sensations are more muted; they can't possibly feel the same sense of risk as us. But they know what time of year it is, and they know what's at stake. They know that if they were only going to watch one hockey game all year, they could do a lot worse than to watch this one.

The bad guys score right off the hop, and all the energy is sucked out of the living room at the same rate as in the Bell Centre. Groans and sighs and cries of "Fuck's sake" and "What the fuck??" There are exchanged glances of commiseration and a cacophony of judgements. Amir and I flail our bodies to hammer home our incredulity. Like the worst kind of hockey parents, we shake our heads ruefully, knowing this was always going to happen. We also know that time is running out. We know that, even if we get into the playoffs, our chances are slim at best, but this is why we watch; this is the whole point. So we want to make it, we want to win, and we're down two goals. We cannot afford this.

Neither George nor Wade has a dog in this fight, but as good Canadian boys, they have played hockey all their lives and understand that this was nothing more than a fuck-up, an aberrant forgetting of the fundamentals that are drilled into you from the age of nine. It was a fuck-up, but not necessarily a portent of doom. "Lot of hockey left," George says. I know he's wrong—there isn't much time left at all—but it's comforting nonetheless, and it sparks the pilot light of hope. And no sooner does that encouraging platitude leave George's lips than a flurry of activity draws our attention to the bad guys' net. It's all so helter-skelter and simultaneous that we are almost surprised by the goal light. I'm not sure what the hell happened, but I know the ref is pointing at the right net and the Bell Centre is cheering, so we must have scored. The living room erupts in celebration. The Habs fans are happy; the rest are happy to be here. I don't actually care if the goal was pretty or not, and I'll have the next minute's worth of replays to either gush over it or just nod at it. Either way, we scored, and the goal was good, and we've cut our deficit in half. Fifteen minutes left in the third.

We know the score; we remember what happened in the first two periods. Just as we remember what has happened throughout the season leading up to this moment, just as we remember everything we've lived before tonight. These memories are all equally meaningless. There is nothing but what's in front of us and what's to come. The living room is a kaleidoscope of smells and energies. We ate supper two hours ago, and some of us have been smoking dope since then, and for three-quarters of the room, the night is social more than anything else. For those of us who are connected to the events on the TV, the energy is tense and fleeting, and everything has consequences. We inch forward subconsciously, we dart up and pace about, but our eyes never leave the screen.

One of our guys gives up the puck in the neutral zone, and just like that, the bad guys are in our end, assuming their positions like it's a drill. We are on the back foot, always on the back foot, and we scramble to keep pace. It is our pace that has defined us, for better or worse, since the beginning. Our pace is the source of our greatest victories and our biggest fuck-ups. In this case, we took to the neutral zone in disjointed, anemic strides usually reserved for line changes, and now we find ourselves being forechecked and emasculated in our own neighbourhood. The bad guys pass the puck about like they're on the power play, and what would be frustrating on a regular night is now horrifying with the season on the line. The puck is rocketed from the blue line, but our goalie gets a piece of it, and it caroms into the corner, where it's pounced on. And all of a sudden there is a mass of bodies thrashing on each other in anger until the coveted black disc squirts free, almost of its own volition, and skips over to the blue paint. In an instant, the scrum in the corner becomes the scrum at our net, and our goalie is being harried and hacked at by a mini hell of composite sticks.

The bottom drops out, and we are hijacked by vertigo. Our hands fly to our faces, and we can't bear to watch, but know that we have to. Twenty-one thousand, two hundred and seventy-three sets of lungs gasp for air at the Bell Centre. Our goalie is less a goalie than a bouncer, defying physics, and he is meeting expectations. He knows this is the job. He knows that if he can't do this now, he might as well never do it. He knows it's this or nothing. Every threatening swat is met with an equal rebuttal, until finally our goalie grabs hold of the puck with everything in him and takes to the ice, and for what feels like a year but is really only like three seconds at most, we all wait for the ref to blow his whistle. And he does, and we can cheer.

"Holy fuck"s and applause all around. The Bell Centre goes hard and defiant in their appreciation of our goalie. It's not over—nowhere near over—but he did what he had to do when he had to do it, and we are still in this fight. The TV announcers echo the sentiments of the living room as we all watch replays of what just happened. "Save of the year," I opine, with complete confidence and sincerity, well aware that this is maybe the third or fourth time I've said these words this season. The living room agrees, or at least acknowledges that it wasn't just happenstance or luck or a product of the high-stakes atmosphere of fighting for your post-season life; this was actually impressive. It wasn't just one good save, but a sincerely Herculean sequence of efforts, and because of it, our hole isn't any deeper.

And now we are forced to watch a bunch of commercials, because that's the cruel reality of being a North American sports fan. We don't have to suffer the indignity of having our favourite jerseys all fucked up by being covered in random ads, but we pay the potentially far higher price of having momentum constantly interrupted by forced breaks in play in order to satisfy advertisers. The ads-on-jerseys thing is crass, but at least it doesn't have any tangible effect on performance or the outcome of a game, like being forced to let Tie Domi try to sell me long-distance coverage does.

We come back from our mandatory break and take stock of the situation before us. Like middle-aged men all of a sudden appreciating the finite nature of mortality, we stare at the score and the clock; we know that we are still down a goal and there is now only ten minutes left in our season. With a faceoff in our end, with the wolves at our door, we stand tall, and the puck is forced away, and just like that, we're on a one-on-one breakaway, and this time of year always feels special, and this could be one of those moments. Someone mutters "Oh shit" under their breath, and we all raise our eyebrows like dogs seeing our masters. We all hope for the same outcome, and we get it: our guy dips in and backhands it through their goalie's legs and the red light goes off. The Bell Centre goes ballistic and so does the living room. In an instant we are all on our feet, our hands in the air or on our heads. This wasn't a garbage goal like the first one. This one was all finesse; the puck went exactly where our guy wanted it to go. And the game is all tied up with eight minutes left.

Elation soon turns to cautious optimism, because we haven't won and the game isn't over. Still, we can't help it; we're beaming. This is an itch that can be scratched by nothing else; this is a very specific kind of excitement, the right blend of history, possibility, and consequences. This is the stuff of memory and why we suffer through low-scoring regulation draws against the Panthers in February. This is stirred blood, and collective intent. This is the answer to "Why hockey?" This is ours; all are welcome, but this is ours.

The ref assembles the cast of characters at centre ice for a reset, and there is a scattering of claps throughout the living room. We are sharpening, waking up, and tuning in. We're still in this thing. They know it in the Bell Centre. It's not time for "Ole, ole, ole," but it is most certainly time for a "Go Habs Go," and that's what happens, the chant quickly consuming the building. It is militant, and impassioned, and rousing. It is the same chant we have heard countless times all season, for every season of our lives, and yet the sound is different. It can change, depending on context. We know, in the pits of our stomachs, the difference between the relentless cheerleading of the relentlessly hopeful and the war cry of a proud city fighting for its life.

The play continues, informed by the last goal. It's quicker, angrier, more vital. There is none of the tentativeness or caution that comes when both teams are scared shitless of conceding a goal. No, this is history beckoning the ambitions of young men. Everybody out there knows what they want and are working their asses off to get it. There's a collision with worse intentions than results that quickly morphs into a scrum along the boards, which quickly morphs into one of our guys getting the puck free and saucering it over to another of our guys. And just like that, it happens—what countless times before yielded little more than frustration and lament for the past: we get a two-on-one that results in a goal. We take the lead.

Because of course we do. We wouldn't be the Habs if we were completely without hope or pride. We wouldn't be the Habs if we weren't annually given a toxic reminder of how awesome we were, once upon a time. We wouldn't be the Habs if we were run right through. It's that hope, that toxic bit of success, that keeps the wins meaningful and the losses painful, and God help us, it always makes us cocky. All of a sudden the Bell Centre is a different building. It's loud as fuck and full of swagger, like Henry V's archers at Agincourt. The living room is full of open jaws, and impressed ohhhhs and oooohs, and the Habs fans are smiling amongst ourselves because anything can happen and we usually find a way to defy odds and inspire hope. Even if it's only to make an inevitable defeat that much harder to stomach.

And of course, we go to a commercial for Tim Hortons' new extreme bacon wrap thing, and I decide to run upstairs to piss super-quick. I'm annoyed at the intrusion, annoyed at capitalism, and annoyed that the apparent omnipotence of Tim Hortons commercials is matched only by their commitment to being as voiceless as possible. I would rather no joke at all than what's in those things. No joke would be better than a dad winking at his twenty-something daughter about eating something he thinks is bad for him but she knows is healthy because Tim Hortons makes Canada safe, or whatever happens in any Tim Hortons commercial. I finish pissing and think about how much I love Tim Hortons' donuts, and then about how nauseous their breakfast sandwiches seem to make me, and then I remember there's a hockey game happening and bolt downstairs just in time for the faceoff.

Somebody is saying something about how shitty *Murdoch Mysteries* is when my eyes go to the game clock and I realize that we are potentially just four minutes away from going to the playoffs. I articulate this fact to the living room, punctuated with a "Holy fuck," and then quickly feel guilty, like I'd said "Macbeth" or, worse, "shutout." God agrees and we take a fucking very stupid penalty for delay of game and I, of course, blame myself. I am annoyed with God, but I get it. I'd have done the same thing to me if I were Him. Regardless, our schmuck goes to the box, and I am instantly engulfed in dread. All of the bluster and small-guy swagger farts away, and we're right back to jaded, cynical square one. I look at the room. "Oy." I have a very bad feeling about this penalty kill.

Our goalie decided to be awesome right when he needed to be, and it feels like the awesome will continue through this last stand, but he's not the one I'm worried about. It's almost never the goalie. I'm worried about all of our tactical deficiencies, and the size disparity. I'm worried about us already being outshot throughout the entirety of this season and my life. I'm worried about God's sardonic sense of humour and the fact that we have made a tradition out of clenching defeat from the jaws of victory, and just generally fucking ourselves over at times of great importance.

This is when the vertigo returns, and hundreds of thousands of fans all subconsciously inch forward as if proximity or focus will affect what happens on the ice. This is when anxious butterflies blitzkrieg our stomachs. This is when our helplessness as passive observers is most palpable. This is when the stakes have been distilled to simplicity, and there are only two outcomes. This is the gravity, the risk, that makes everything else consequential.

There are only two minutes left in this game, potentially in this regular season, and everything is happening quickly and life is fragile and we are dying every day, and yet, somehow, this power play seems like it goes on forever. The bad guys pass the puck back and forth like the Harlem Globetrotters. Their passes, their positioning, their ambition—all of it seems tighter than ours ever did. Whenever we are on the power play, it feels improvised, handmade, like the boys are forever struggling to keep pace with events beyond their control. Every other team feels dominant and practised. Like these guys.

I'm about to throw out a "Fuck's sake" when they shoot and, of course, our goalie stands tall. It is a brief, finite victory that we instantly forget as the puck bounces away and is quickly reclaimed by the bad guys. Everyone in the living room is as tuned to the game as the Bell Centre is. Everyone is watching. Some of us still give more of a shit than others, but we are all aware that stuff is on the line. This is our fighter, bleeding out and leaning on the ropes. Not dead, but in terrible danger. Our hearts are in our throats. All of the postmodern existentialist criticisms I have of this team, or this league, or the servile nature of the Canadian-American dynamic, all of it feels miles away. In this moment, everything is simple. I know what I want, what I don't want, and what I am afraid of. I want my team to survive, I don't want them to allow a goal, and I am afraid that's exactly what they will do.

And they do. The bad guys pounce on a rebound and bend our net. The red light turns on, the ref points. It's like being rear-ended out of a stoplight daydream. In mere seconds, the air is sucked out of the Bell Centre and the living room. We swear as we facepalm. Of course this happened. Of course it did. The goal smarts. Not the acrid, burning pain of a go-ahead goal, but the frustrating, prodigal ache of feeling predestination at work. We have not been dominant in this game, and most of our successes have been jerry-rigged. We have propped a window open with a plastic ladle we knew wasn't strong enough, but so long as the window stayed open, we never felt inclined to address the issue properly, and now, as it slams shut, destroying the ladle and fucking up the windowpane, we are pissed but we know we probably deserve this. That's what this feels like. Of course this happened. Of course it did. Because we're us, and we are of Montreal, and Montreal is of Canada. We're not the Yankees, and they don't make movies about Canada.

And just like that, we are, effectively, back to the start of the game, back to zero. The bad guys have tied it up, all but negating everything that's come before. The previous goals have no relevance beyond the esoteric question of "Do we have another in us?" as if there is a specific, finite number of goals that can be scored during any one hockey game. That number doesn't exist, but reason and precedent and logic tell us that, more often than not, a game will feature five goals or less. So, as the clock ticks down, we know that not only are we running out of time, we might also be running out of options.

We are tired and have been fighting uphill all night, and now we have one more reason to be in our heads. We have found a way to get properly inspired, and productive, on a few occasions tonight. We pulled it together and looked like a hockey team, but felt like we were defying the odds every time. It feels like we missed our chance to cash out and quit while we were ahead. It feels like the man is coming around.

The end is near. We are hostages of the moment and unable to look away. Time pours itself down the drain as my favourite hockey team flutters about the ice, caught between the desire for victory and the fear of defeat. These emotions cancel themselves out, and I don't think we will score before the end of regulation. The bad guys might, but I don't think we will. I think we are fighting for survival, and we'll hope for the best in OT. I think we are shell-shocked and too self-aware for our own good. I think we've been a cornered animal for almost three decades, and have forgotten what confidence feels like. I think we remember too much, and it's driving us mad. I think we take too much responsibility and owe too much to too many cultural debtors. I think the bad guys are about to score again.

Our goalie stands tall. Again. The puck has been a hot potato for him all night, and again it flutters away just as time does, and we are now less than a minute away from the end of regulation and anything can happen. Anything won't happen, but it can. We probably won't score, just as, if we somehow find a way to win tonight, we probably won't survive the first round. Even if we do, we probably won't survive the second, and so on and so forth, and most of our chutzpah was gone before I was born. The puck skips along the boards, but we're too scared to risk being out of position and the bad guys get it. Again. We hold fast, because that's all we can do. We embrace what's strongest and most successful in ourselves, and we ride that until we can do so no longer. For the Habs, it's our goalie. Always our goalie. And so, when the chips are down and time is running out, and seasons, contracts, and pride are all on the line, we fall back and rest the bulk of our aspirations on our goalie. He steals games for us, so we hope to steal seasons with him. We fire the puck up-ice, hoping to ice ourselves into OT.

But one of our guys collects it and becomes a helpless vassal of daring. His sweater and the banners above his head do all the work for him. He channels ambition and every player that's ever worn that sweater, and he finds enough energy to skate forward and take on the world. He is not playing it safe, and he is playing for himself as much as anyone, because that's how it works. We can't see the bench, but I know our coaches aren't happy. Their job is following the smart money, and this is a crapshoot. Our guy holds on to the puck and finds a way through the defender and past the blue line. Thirty seconds left.

We are, all of us, on our feet now. This is it. This is what we came for. This is what it looks like. This is fandom, in all of its complicated, beautiful ugliness. We pray, and adopt the demeanour of scared children waiting to be told everything is okay. We know our guy should have just dumped the puck and gotten off the ice. We know he probably won't score, but holy fuck, do we ever want him to. We have no choice anyway, so we can do little but hope for the best. It's one on one.

Our guy against their goalie. History is on our side; reality is on theirs. Either way, I know it's almost over.

Our guy holds on longer than expected and then cuts to the left, arcing into some sort of spinning thing. Because of course he does. Because we, the Habs, are a team of individuals, and so are our successes and defeats. He should just shoot, but instead, he must flourish. It's stupid and vainglorious, but if he pulls it off, we will all love him for it. Forever. He knows this and so do we, and again, we have no choice, so we can do little but hope for the best. Their goalie stays put and our guy has a chance to finish his spin. He comes out of it already lifting his stick off the ice. The goalie's reflexes force him forward and our guy shoots—

And it doesn't matter if it goes in or not. It doesn't matter if the fates somehow deem us interesting enough to squeak into the playoffs. It doesn't matter if we somehow Cinderella ourselves through the first or even second round. It doesn't matter if we somehow make it through the Eastern Conference finals and get to the fucking Cup. It doesn't matter, because all that really matters is winning the Stanley Cup, and anything less than that is just methadone. Because we are of Montreal and these are the Habs. Because we don't take pride in all those times we made it to the Cup but didn't bring it home. We don't talk with reverence about the boys who brought us to Calgary, only to have Lanny McDonald and Doug Gilmour best us in six games. Other teams can and do. Other teams have to, because what the fuck else can they take pride in? What other history do they have?

This season will end slightly north or south of where every season without a Cup ends: defeat and summertime melancholy. It doesn't matter. And yet it does. It matters as much as we want it to. It matters because we choose to let it matter, and if we connect ourselves to our team, then their victories—all of their victories, large or small—are our victories too. So even if I understand that this is all horseshit and that there are bigger fish to fry, I will always feel that it isn't, and that the Habs are as important as anything in my life. They will fail and lose seasons before the preseason has even begun. They will inspire and make mini legends as they chase the Grail and lose their lives to the quest. They will seduce and love, and then break my heart. They will trick me into cockiness and harangue me with self-evident failure. They will win and they will lose, and maybe one day they will bring the Cup back to its rightful home.

This season will end, as all seasons end, and soon another will begin anew, and I will go through all of this all over again, and again and again. This season is every season, and I am all but completely helpless to divorce myself from its events. Even if I wasn't, I wouldn't have it any other way.

I was born into this.

I live it still.

To you from failing hands we throw
The torch; be yours to hold it high.

THE NIGHT WILL TAKE US ALL

And the sentient air to kill for all watchers
And the broken night for our blood; no context found

Force your will upon the devil's will
Burn holy through cities of the damned
Radiate God with your every darling tremble; Redeemer

Young hearts hunt hearts
And all the nights last forever for us
You and I and no one else

Truth in all things
Truth and exaltation

And all the world's artifice is earnest
And everything you hate is wrong
And they will always never beat us

For the night will take us all

ACKNOWLEDGEMENTS

ABOVE ALL, I am very grateful for, and thankful to, my mother, Robyne Ropell-Baruchel, without whom I would not only not exist but would probably be homeless or in jail or going back and forth between the two. When I was a kid, my mum told me that just because most grown-ups hate their jobs didn't mean I had to. She told me to "pick something you would do for free and then find a way to get paid to do it." She also taught me to be compassionate and forthright, and to help others when I can. These have been, and continue to be, the guiding principles of my life, and they are the result of being raised by the best mother in the world.

I would be very much remiss were I not to thank my sister, Taylor, for being smarter than me and for refusing to give up on the world, and for a loyalty that knows almost no parallel. I say "almost" because I would also like to thank my stepfather,

ACKNOWLEDGEMENTS

Cliff, for proving to me every day that heroism is real and that there are still good men left.

Words can't even begin to describe the debt I owe my lady, Rebecca-Jo Dunham. Suffice it to say that she is the best person I know, and I am a better person every day that I get to share life with her.

Thank you to my friends, which is really just another way of saying thank you to the surrogate members of my family. Amir, Evan Dubinsky, George, Jesse, Jason, Andrew, Wade, Jacob, George, Ricky, Cierra, Krumholtz, Evan Goldberg, Liosha, Kris, Aaron, Lauren. You are in this book in ways literal and esoteric. Your solidarities and your spirits keep me alive, and you will forever have me in your corner.

I'd like to give special thanks to the above-mentioned Amir, Amir Nakhjavani, not only for twenty-plus years of friendship but, in particular, for his ceaseless efforts in helping me with this book. Amir is far better educated and much smarter than I am, and he had no reason to review any of this, but I am very fortunate that he did. The book and I are better for it.

Thanks to my managers, Marc Hamou and Willie Mercer, who have, for some insane reason, chosen to believe in me and represent me for almost twenty years. They have protected me and inspired me, and they contradict everything I hate about the entertainment business. They are the older brothers I never had, and I would be nowhere without them. The same can be said of my lawyer, Jamie Feldman, and my agents, Steve Smooke and Simon Green, at Creative Artists, all of whom have also defied reason and continue to represent me. I don't know why they do it, and I often feel bad that they do, but I am really happy that they do.

A massive thank you to my editor, Jim Gifford, whose guidance, patience, and enthusiasm have forced my disparate rambling essays into a cohesive work. He had no reason to believe that I could write this thing, and yet he did. And because Jim believed I could do it, I believed I could do it. And then I did it. Jim has had the unenviable task of suffering my "creative process" for the better part of two years and has only ever given terrific notes and motivated me to write the best book that I could. This book doesn't exist without him. Nor does it exist without HarperCollins Canada, who also had no reason to believe that this would be a thing I could do. I'm touched and honoured that they did, and I have endeavoured to repay their confidence in me with this work. A special thank you to Doug Richmond, as well, for his thoughts early on in the process.

I would like to thank the people of Montreal for their joie de vivre, their pride, and their righteous defiance. And, finally, I'd like to thank the people of Toronto, who are well aware of what a snobby little shithead from Montreal I am and yet continue to make me feel welcome. Montreal is my home, but now so is Toronto, and as much as I make fun of it, the truth is, I really think this is a nice place to live.